DK EYEWITNESS TRAVEL

TOP 10
SICILY

ELAINE TRIGIANI

Top 10 Sicily Highlights

The Top 10 of Everything

CONTENTS

Sicily
Area by Area

Streetsmart

Within each Top 10 list in this book, no hierarchy of quality or popularity is implied. All 10 are, in the editor's opinion, of roughly equal merit.

Front cover and spine *The medieval town of Cefalù, with its striking cathedral*
Back cover *A boat on Isola Bella beach, Taormina*
Title page *Agrigento Temple of Concordia*

Welcome to
Sicily

Sicily has always been an intriguing crossroads of cultures and civilizations. At the tip of the Italian peninsula, its strategic position in the Mediterranean sea attracted visitors and invaders alike. Nowadays, the wealth of ancient sights, stunning natural beauty and family-friendly beaches make Sicily an ideal and unforgettable holiday destination. With Eyewitness Top 10 Sicily, it's yours to explore.

Over the centuries Sicily has been part of Greater Greece, a Roman province, a Byzantine stronghold, an Arab Caliphate, a Norman kingdom, a pawn for Spain and the Bourbons, and ultimately part of a unified Italy. The vestiges of bygone eras are ever-present, so it is no surprise that the island has developed a powerful identity all of its own – so much so that the great German writer Johann Wolfgang von Goethe said that "without Sicily, Italy creates no image in the soul; here is the key to everything".

Today, Sicily still holds that key: the largest island in the Mediterranean is an explosion of colours and idiosyncrasies that are both enticing and baffling to visitors. But as you stroll past the crumbling ruins, experience the liveliness of the markets as locals go about their everyday business, observe old men playing cards in the town square, and feast on the delectable food the island is renowned for, it is impossible not to be charmed.

Whether you're here for a weekend or a week, our Top 10 guide brings together the best of everything Sicily has to offer, from immaculate beaches and verdant mountains to archaeological treasures and ornate royal palaces. The guide gives you tips throughout, from seeking out what's free to avoiding the crowds, plus seven easy-to-follow itineraries designed to help you visit a clutch of sights in a short space of time. Add inspiring photography and detailed maps, and you've got the essential pocket-sized travel companion. **Enjoy the book, and enjoy Sicily.**

Clockwise from top: **Cefalù; La Scala dei Turchi; church of San Cataldo, Palermo; Favignana; Ten Girls in Bikinis mosaic at Villa Romana del Casale; Stromboli; Temple E, Selinute**

Exploring Sicily

Given its size and number of sites, it's impossible to see all of Sicily in less than a week. Here we help you maximise your time, with a seven-day itinerary covering the key sights in Sicily, and a two-day itinerary just for the Aeolian Islands.

Seven Days in Sicily

Day ❶

Spend the morning visiting old **Palermo** (see pp12–13) – don't miss the **Palazzo dei Normanni** and the **Cappella Palatina**. Lunch at one of the city's outdoor markets. Take bus 389 from Piazza Indipendenza to the bottom of the town, then walk to **Monreale** (see pp14–15), a glorious church from the Norman era. Marvel at the glittering 12th-century mosaics inside, then explore the adjacent cloisters.

Villa Romana del Casale

Day ❷

Hire a car or take the train to **Segesta** (see p44), the romantic site of the only freestanding limestone temple in Sicily, as well as a 3rd-century BC theatre with stunning views. Head to **Erice** (see p99) and visit the Castle of Venus, then head to Maria Grammatico to buy sweets. Stay the night at Agriturismo Antica Tenuta dei Pignatelli in **Castelvetrano**, "City of Olives and Temples" (see p102).

Day ❸

Drive or take the bus to **Selinunte** (see pp36–9) and see what remains of the mighty Selinus Acropolis. The Valle dei Templi in **Agrigento** (see pp32–5) is home to beautiful temples. The Temple of Concord features a Paleochristian church.

Day ❹

Drive to **Villa Romana del Casale** near Piazza Armerina (see pp30–31). View Roman-era mosaics, including the famous Ten Girls in Bikinis. Drive to **Noto** (see pp28–9) and spend the afternoon exploring this Baroque town. Stay in **Syracuse** (see pp24–7) at the Grand Hotel Minareto (see p144).

The Temple of Concordia, Agrigento, dates from 430 BC but is remarkably intact.

Key
— Two-day Itinerary
— Seven-day Itinerary

0 km   30
0 miles 30

The Aeolian Islands each have their own unique character and beauty.

way to the beautiful Teatro Antico. Make sure you take part in the traditional *passeggiata* (evening stroll). Before leaving Sicily, visit the beaches at lovely **Giardini Naxos** *(see p109)*, just below Taormina, where Greek colonization began.

Two Days on the Aeolian Islands

Day ❶
MORNING
From **Milazzo** go to the Aeolian Islands *(see pp16–17)*. Disembark at **Lipari** for the Museo Archeologico Regionale Eoliano *(see p51)*.
AFTERNOON
Travel to the eastern isles with Avventurisole Viaggi Eolie (www.eolietour.com). Pause on **Panarea**, sample pizza on **Stromboli**, and watch the volcano from the boat.

Day ❷
MORNING
Island hopping starts from **Alicudi**. Take the hydrofoil and head eastwards to **Filicudi**, famous for its lentils and capers. Next it's east to Salina, where Malvasia grapes are harvested.
AFTERNOON
Back on Lipari, visit the stunning Cava del Pomice, a former pumice rock quarry, now a beach. Finish the day with a drink at Il Piccolo Bar on Via Marina Garibaldi, Canneto.

Day ❺
Syracuse was once the most powerful city of the Mediterranean – its Greek Theatre held 20,000 people. Don't miss the Ear of Dionysius in the Latomia del Paradiso and the Temple of Apollo. Explore the beautiful island of Ortygia. Take in the Piazza Duomo, then visit the Cathedral, built within the Temple of Minerva. Finish at Castello Maniace.

Day ❻
Visit **Mount Etna** *(see pp20–21)* from Piano Provenzana. Take the cable car at Rifugio Sapienza, and once you've arrived at base camp, hop into one of the jeeps that shuttle visitors to the top. Take in the Valle del Bove, a valley filled with lava flow. Stop in at a beekeeper's and buy some honey.

Day ❼
Taormina *(see pp18–19)* is home to Italy's glitterati. Visit Palazzo Corvaja and the Odeon, before making your

Top 10 Sicily Highlights

Temple of Juno, Valley of the Temples, Agrigento

🔟 Sicily Highlights

The island of Sicily is Italy's largest region and its most varied. There are offshore islands, cliffs and beaches, rugged mountains, rolling wheatfields and volcanoes. Sicily's history is also of note. The Greeks, Romans, Byzantines and Normans all left their mark on the island.

Palermo ①
The island capital's history is best seen in its architecture – medieval quarters with crumbling Baroque churches, exquisite Arab-Norman churches and precious Art Nouveau *palazzi (see pp12–13)*.

San Vito lo Capo
Trapani
Egadi Islands
Segesta
Marsala
Val di Mázara
Chiusa Sclafani
Selinunte ⑩
Sciacca
Palermo ①
Monreale ②
San Cipirello
Corleone
Cerda
Alia
Caltabellotta
Eraclea Minoa
Agrigento ⑨

Monreale ②
A spectacular Norman monument, the mosaic cycle at Monreale Cathedral is a wonder of the medieval world *(see pp14–15)*.

Taormina ④
Sicily's first resort has welcomed visitors for centuries. The town offers breathtaking views, an ancient theatre, and cafés and terraces overlooking the sea *(see pp18–19)*.

Aeolian Islands ③
These seven volcanic islands offer a live volcano, black lava beaches, and food and wines flavoured by the sun *(see pp16–17)*.

5 Mount Etna

This, the largest and most active volcano in Europe, looms powerfully over eastern Sicily *(see pp20–21)*.

6 Syracuse

This once mighty Greek colony and rival to Athens is today a thriving modern city. Traces of its former glory include a Baroque cathedral and a Greek theatre *(see pp24–7)*.

7 Noto

Destroyed by an earthquake in 1693, Noto was rebuilt during the 1700s, when the Baroque style was at its height *(see pp28–9)*.

8 Villa Romana del Casale

The extensive mosaic decorations of this luxurious Roman villa are the best preserved of their kind in the world *(see pp30–31)*.

9 Agrigento

The famed Valle dei Templi is home to ruined Greek temples that stand, as they have for 2,500 years, against a backdrop of the distant sea *(see pp32–5)*.

10 Selinunte

Another of Sicily's remarkable ancient sites, the romantic remains of Greek Selinus reign spectacularly from a promontory high above the sea. This is the largest archaeological park in Europe *(see pp36–9)*.

🔟 ⭐ Palermo

When the Phoenicians founded Palermo in 735 BC, they named it Zyz ("flower"), such was the beauty of its verdant hills, dotted with fruit trees and native flora. This greenery is still visible, especially along the paths that wind their way up to the former Phoenician fortress, now the Palazzo dei Normanni. Palermo is now Sicily's buzzing artistic centre, home to grand opera houses, tiny theatres and avant-garde museums. There's plenty of culture, whether you're visiting the former church of San Giovanni degli Eremiti or meandering past the delightfully stuccoed Oratorio di San Lorenzo.

1 Cathedral
Founded in 1185, the cathedral **(right)** is an eclectic mix of architectural styles. Admire the 12-century apse, the porphyry royal tombs, the crypt and the treasury housing Empress Constance's crown.

2 San Cataldo
This church **(above)** is an example of the Arab-Norman architecture that flourished across Sicily under Norman control. Its roof has three red domes and Arab-style parapets.

3 Oratorio di San Lorenzo
With a white stucco interior by the sculptor Giacomo Serpotta, the 16th-century oratory housed a Caravaggio painting, until it was stolen in 1969.

Palermo

4 Palazzo dei Normanni
The royal palace is testament to the city's Arab-Norman heritage. Its Punic foundations, the dazzling mosaics of La Stanza di Ruggero and the Torre Gioaria (Arab wind tower) embody its long history.

5 Palazzo Steri
Grafitti on the walls serves as a poignant reminder that this was the seat of the Inquisition in the 17th century.

⑦ Cappella Palatina

Commissioned in 1129 by Roger II, the chapel **(left)** in the Palazzo dei Normanni harmoniously combines western and Arab styles. The Arab ceiling is painted with animals and greenery. It also shows a Christ Pantocrator, produced by Byzantine masters using gold and silver tesserae, offering his blessing from the cupola and the apse.

⑧ La Zisa

This castle, built in the 12th century by Arab masons, is inspired by Moorish architecture. Its name comes from *al-Azīz*, meaning "splendid".

⑨ San Giovanni degli Eremiti

Founded in 1132, and set amid lush gardens, San Giovanni **(above)** was the richest monastery in Sicily. Five red domes, typical of Arab style, mark the exterior, while the interior of the church has only remnants of its original decoration.

⑥ La Martorana

Santa Maria dell' Ammiraglio **(below)** is called La Martorana after 12th-century nun Eloisa Martorana, who used to decorate the church with mosaics *(see p91)*.

THE NORMANS IN SICILY

In 1061 Norman soldier Roger de Hauteville took advantage of internal Arab conflict in order to invade the island with a small group of crusaders. He was the first of five powerful Norman kings who, over the next century, turned Sicily into a well-run and wealthy monarchy. By 1266, they left behind an island endowed with splendid buildings and an exotic culture that blended western and Arab influences.

NEED TO KNOW

Cathedral: **MAP K5**; Via Vittorio Emanuele; open 7am–7pm Mon–Sat, 8am–1pm & 4–7pm Sun & public hols; adm €3 for the crypt, treasury, royal tombs

Palazzo dei Normanni: **MAP J6**; Piazza Indipendenza; open 8am–5:40pm Mon–Sat, 8:15am–1pm Sun (royal apartments closed Tue–Thu when parliament is in session); adm €8.50 Fri–Mon & hols, €7 Tue–Thu

Cappella Palatina: **MAP J6**; open 8:15am–5pm Mon–Sat, 8:15am–1pm Sun & hols; adm included in ticket for Palazzo dei Normanni

⑩ Palazzo della Cuba

Constructed in 1180 for William II of Sicily as his personal recreation pavilion, Palazzo della Cuba was designed by the Arab artists who were still living in the city after the Norman conquest.

TOP 10 ⭐ Monreale

The cathedral at Monreale, high above the fertile Conca d'Oro (Golden Shell), overlooks Palermo. King William II founded the majestic cathedral and Benedictine monastery in 1174, and a medieval village soon grew up around them. Despite its rather austere exterior, inside the cathedral has spectacular decoration, which constitutes the most extensive and important mosaic cycle of its kind in Sicily. The entrance is in Piazza Vittorio Emanuele.

1 Apse Exterior
In contrast to the rest of the exterior, which is relatively plain, the triple apse **(below)** is decorated with intricate stonework that forms interlacing arches of limestone and lava.

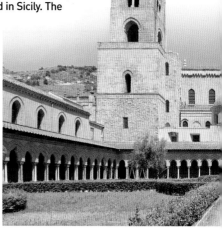

2 Façade
The façade, with a bronze door, is bracketed by two asymmetrical square towers and bears decorative stonework. The front porch is an 18th-century addition.

4 Ceilings
The choir ceiling shows traces of Arab influences with guilded motifs and decorative patterns. The nave ceiling was restored after a fire in 1811.

3 Interior
The interior **(below)** has granite columns with Roman Corinthian capitals supporting around 6,500 sq m (70,000 sq ft) of brilliant mosaics.

5 Side Apse Mosaics

Above the thrones to either side of the main apse are portraits of William II being crowned by Christ himself, and presenting the cathedral to the Madonna, a scene blessed by the hand of God.

8 Nave Mosaics

These Old and New Testament scenes were educational panels for the illiterate parishioners of the time. They include the Creation, Noah's Ark and the Sacrifice of Isaac (above).

9 Apse Mosaic of Christ

The enormous image of the Christ Pantocrator embraces his followers with curved arms and outstretched hands from on high.

10 North Transept

Here visitors can walk on spectacular Cosmati mosaics arranged in intricate patterns, such as the four hares in a circle. Head into the Capella Roano to see some exquisite Baroque craftsmanship.

Floorplan of Monreale

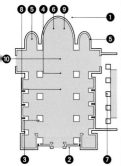

7 Cloister

The calm cloister (above) combines Arab-styled arches, intricately carved capitals decorated with mosaic patterns, and a lovely 12th-century fountain in the geometric garden.

6 Mosaics of Martyr Saints

One of the martyr saints shown is St Thomas à Becket, canonized the year before the church was founded. It is his earliest known portrait.

NEED TO KNOW

MAP C2 ■ Piazza Guglielmo II 1, Monreale ■ 091 6406671 ■ AST buses: from Palermo (Piazza Indipendenza) to Monreale

Cathedral: 8:30am–12:45pm & 2:30–5:30pm daily. Adm €2.50 for south transept, €2 for roof

Cloister: 091 6404403; 9am–7pm Mon–Sat, 9am–1:30pm Sun & public hols. Adm €6

■ Have a coffee or *gelato* at the Bar Baby O' in Piazza Gugliemo before or after your visit.

■ The church is popular for weddings – if one is in progress when you visit, go to the cloisters and gardens first and return to the church after the service has finished.

TOP 10 ⭐ Aeolian Islands

This chain of volcanic islands offers a small-town atmosphere, flavourful cuisine, history and natural beauty. Each of the islands has its own character: Lipari is bright white with pumice; the fertile volcanic soil of Salina grows verdant grapevines and forests with rock formations like mounds of whipped cream; on Vulcano cooled molten lava has left cliffs like rows of elephants' legs. Beaches are powdery grey-white with pumice or black with powdered lava, and the sea is clean, clear and full of marine life.

1 Pollara Beach, Salina

The beach at Pollara **(above)** has large pebbles as well as patches of sand. The water is great for snorkelling, with sea urchins, octopuses and other sea life.

2 Perciato di Pollara, Salina

This stone arch swoops down from the cliff and comes to rest in the sea, creating a natural rock bridge **(below)**. Visitors can get to the breathtaking Perciato via land or sea and then swim around the rocks.

3 Stromboli

A storied Aeolian volcano, Stromboli has been active for over two millennia, spewing sparks and red-hot rocks into the air, although you can only see them at night. Excursions are popular and available from the other islands.

NEED TO KNOW

MAP F1

Museo Archeologico Regionale Eoliano: Via del Castello, Lipari; 090 9880174; 9am–6:30pm daily (to 1:30pm on public hols; winter by appt only). Adm €6

■ It is best to stick to small, unassuming *trattorie* for good food at better prices.

■ The island chain is made up of fragile volcanic stone, so watch out for falling rocks *(caduta massi)*.

4 Museo Archeologico Regionale Eoliano

The museum features items from the islands' Neolithic settlements, as well as impressive Greek and Roman displays **(left)**.

5 Sulphur Emissions, Vulcano

Sulphur emissions still seep from the main crater on Vulcano, and all over the island the vapour rises out of the craggy ground. The earth is a lurid yellow **(below)** and there are many *fanghi* (mudbaths).

OBSIDIAN AND PUMICE

The volcanic by-products obsidian and pumice have played vital roles in Lipari's commerce. The heavy, dense, glass-like black obsidian was crafted into knives and arrowheads in the Neolithic period and was highly valued and widely traded. The quarrying of white, porous pumice was the major industry at Lipari, where the enormous quarries ground the rock for use in a variety of industries worldwide.

9 Alicudi and Filicudi

Tiny Alicudi **(below)** and Filicudi are the furthest-west and least-developed islands of the archipelago. They are perhaps the prettiest of the islands, with a sparse population, few cars and white-washed houses with breezy terraces.

6 Panarea

The tiniest island of the Aeolian archipelago is also its most exclusive. Panarea is known for its coves, clear water, rocky islets and nightlife. It also has a Bronze Age settlement.

7 Pumice Mines, Lipari

Lipari's biggest industry used to be pumice mining, until UNESCO urged the government to stop this industrial exploitation. Pumice is still so plentiful you'll find pieces of it washing up onto beaches, bobbing in the water and on sale in shops.

8 Marina Corta, Lipari

Smaller craft dock here, under this castle rock. In summer it bustles with activity; in winter you will see only the odd fisherman mending his nets.

10 Malvasia delle Lipari

This is the famed wine of the islands. White grapes are cultivated, harvested late and left to shrivel on cane mats before fermentation.

🔟 ⭐ Taormina

On Monte Tauro, with views of the rocky coastline, the blue-green sea and breathtaking Mount Etna, Taormina was founded in 304 BC as a colony of powerful Syracuse. The town endured a typical Sicilian history, falling first to the Romans, then to the Arabs, Normans and Spanish. During the 1800s Taormina became a stop on the Grand Tour and has been host to foreign visitors ever since. With its plethora of restaurants, hotels and shops, beaches and gardens, it is Sicily's most popular holiday destination.

1 Santuario Madonna della Rocca

Affording heavenly views, this 17th-century church was built where a shepherd sheltering from a storm claimed to see the Virgin Mary.

3 Teatro Antico

With a spectacular view as a backdrop, the Greeks built the theatre in the 3rd century BC, but what can be seen today **(right)** was refurbished by the Romans in the 1st century AD.

2 Mazzarò

Below Taormina are a few lovely beaches, such as Mazzarò. Tiny Isola Bella nearby **(above)** is linked to the coast by a strip of sand.

4 Piazza Vittorio Emanuele

The Palazzo Corvaja, is an architectural mix of Arab, Norman and Catalan Gothic elements. The Baroque Santa Caterina church is backed by the ruins of a Roman Odeon that is free to visit.

5 Piazza del Duomo

The Baroque fountain in the piazza bears a centaur, the symbol of Taormina, here atypically female. The 13th-century Chiesa Madre is dedicated to San Nicolò.

NEED TO KNOW

MAP H3

Teatro Antico: Via Teatro Greco 12; 094 223220; 9am–7pm daily. Adm €10

■ After visiting the Teatro Antico, stop at the Wunderbar Café (Piazza IX Aprile 7) for a drink and some people-watching.

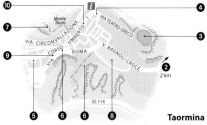

Taormina

8 Villa Comunale Gardens

With great views down to Giardini Naxos *(see p109)*, these well-tended gardens **(left)** have palm and banana trees, birds of paradise, exotic plants, many whimsical buildings and a monument to Taormina's sailors.

FAMOUS VISITORS

The key names that have enjoyed Taormina's beauty include: Greek king Pyrrhus (318–272 BC); Norman conqueror Count Roger *(see p42)*; German poet Johann Wolfgang von Goethe (1749–1832); English novelist D. H. Lawrence (1885–1930); American playwright Tennessee Williams (1911–83); English author Roald Dahl (1916–90); and Hollywood movie stars Elizabeth Taylor and Richard Burton.

10 Corso Umberto I

Locals make their *passeggiata* (nightly stroll) on the Corso **(above)**, starting at Porta Messina, crossing lively piazzas with *gelaterie*, bars, shops and crowds to end at Porta Catania.

6 Piazza IX Aprile

This is a rather lovely square, where you are spoilt for choice between the pretty sea views and people-watching at the many outdoor cafés. The Wunderbar plays live music in the evenings.

9 Borgo Medievale

The clock tower **(below)** is the gateway to the medieval part of town. The Corso is narrower here, and while the shops are the usual mix of clothing and souvenirs, the shop fronts have kept their medieval character.

7 Castelmola Walk

Take the Via Crucis path to the summit of Monte Tauro from Via Circonvallazione to enjoy the spectacular views and the ruins of the medieval castle.

🔟 ⭐ Mount Etna

Mount Etna, Europe's largest volcano, with many craters and a height of 3,330 m (10,925 ft), remains one of the most active in the world. To the Greeks, it was home to Hephaestus, god of fire; Arabs knew it as Mongibello (Mountain of Mountains). Today, the Parco dell'Etna encompasses the volcano, where farmers produce wine, honey and fruit in the lava-rich soil. It offers breathtaking views, great hiking and, in season, skiing, and the occasional eruption of red sparks and lava. In 2013, Mount Etna became a UNESCO World Heritage Site.

3 Visitor Centre
Visitors can find a trained guide at the Rifugio Sapienza Etna Sud **(left)**. Walks start at the top cable-car station; they vary in length and can sometimes include a jeep transfer to see the lava flows.

DRAMATIC ERUPTIONS
In 1928, lava wiped out Mascali. The 1950s, 60s and 70s endangered Milo, Fornazzo, Zafferana Etnea and Sant'Alfio. An eruption in 1979 killed nine tourists. Between 1991 and 1993, concrete blocks were dropped from helicopters to stop lava near Zafferana Etnea. Between 1999 and 2002, ash covered Catania. Lava flows in 2001 and 2002 destroyed visitor centres and the cable-car station at Etna Sud.

1 Circumetnea Train
From Catania, this quirky, narrow-gauge private railway passes Adrano (site of a Saracen bridge), Bronte (with several pistachio farms), Randazzo (to see Lake Gurrida and lava flows) and Linguaglossa (site of an open-air mural museum).

2 Hiking
Hikes on lower slopes and towards the crater are possible, safety permitting. Tourist offices provide maps and guides.

Mount Etna

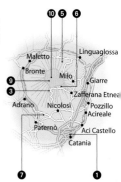

4 Vegetation

Etna is home to a variety of trees, from oak and chestnut in lower areas to pine and birch higher up. Wild flowers, including violets **(above)**, flourish in the soil.

5 Slopes to the East and North

These slopes are home to the *Betula aetnensis* birch, unique to Mount Etna, and, in Sant'Alfio, the *Castagno dei Cento Cavalli* (Chestnut of 100 Horses), one of the oldest and largest trees in the world. Lava flows have formed caves and grottoes, used as shelters and ice stores.

6 Valle del Bove

This crater was created by a collapse of the volcano wall. It covers 7 km by 5 km (4.5 miles by 3 miles) and has walls more than 1,000 m (3,000 ft) high. In 1991 a vent opened, releasing lava into the valley for two years.

7 Slopes to the West and South

Small volcanic cones and cultivated crops, notably pistachio, cover the western slopes. Recent lava flows can be seen on the south slopes.

9 Summit Craters

The summit height is constantly in flux due to the mounting volcanic debris ejected during explosions and the frequent landslides.

8 Fauna

Weasels, wildcats, foxes and birds such as the peregrine falcon survive in wooded areas. At the top, the only fauna to be found are ladybirds.

10 Lava Flows

Molten lava **(above)** is more than 500° C (930° F). In some places, the constant flow, 2 m (6.5 ft) underfoot, causes the snow to melt.

Dramatic slopes of Mount Etna

🔟 ⭐ Syracuse

Founded in 733 BC by Corinthian settlers, Syracusae became one of the first Greek colonies on the island. It attained wealth and power, commissioned important buildings and works of art, and founded sub-colonies, extending its territory through warfare to become the strongest city in the Mediterranean. The ancient city was several times the size of Syracuse today and was divided into five zones: Epipolae, Akradina, Neapolis, Tyche and the original settlement of Ortygia.

1 Castello Maniace
Situated at the tip of Ortygia, Castello Maniace **(above)** is a fortress commissioned by Frederick II. Its 13th-century interiors are almost perfectly intact.

2 Altar of Hieron II
Hieron II built this vast altar, the largest in Magna Graecia, around 225 BC and dedicated it to Zeus Eleutherios, the god of freedom.

3 Catacombs of San Giovanni
Throughout these vast limestone catacombs are burial chambers of various sizes to accommodate children, adults or families.

4 Latomia del Paradiso
Stone from this *latomia* (quarry) was used for the construction of Syracuse. Within the quarry is the *Orecchio di Dioniso* (the Ear of Dionysius) cavern **(below)**, which was probably named because it has a large opening that resembles a human ear.

NEED TO KNOW

MAP H5

Parco Archeologico (Altar of Hieron II, Greek Theatre and Roman Ampitheatre): Viale Augusto; 093 166206; summer: 9am–7:30pm daily (to 4:30pm during theatre season). Adm €10

Catacombs of San Giovanni: Piazza S Giovanni; 093 164694; from 9:30am daily (closing times vary, closed for lunch). Adm €8

Museo Archeologico Regionale Paolo Orsi: Viale

Teocrito 66; 093 1464511; 9am–7pm Tue–Sat, 9am–1pm Sun & hols. Adm €8

Castello Euriala: 8 km (5 miles) from Syracuse; 093 1711773; 2:30pm–7:30pm Mon, 8:30am–1:45pm Tue–Sun. Adm €4

■ The cafés on Ortygia come alive at sundown. Enjoy the cool sea breeze and relaxed atmosphere.

■ Combined tickets (€13.50) are available for the Museo Archeologico Regionale Paolo Orsi and Parco Archeologico.

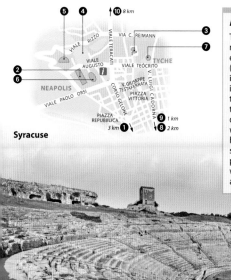

Syracuse

ARCHIMEDES

The renowned inventor, mathematician and engineer Archimedes (287–212 BC) was born in Syracuse. Among his important discoveries is the Archimedes Principle, the study of an object's displacement of its own weight in water. He put his other inventions, such as catapults and pulleys, to use in war when he was military advisor to King Hieron II.

5 **Greek Theatre**
Begun in the 6th century BC, the Greek Theatre **(above)** became the largest in Sicily. Many of Aeschylus's tragedies were first staged here, including *Prometheus Bound*.

6 **Roman Amphitheatre**
This Roman arena was built during the 3rd century AD and is one of the largest of its kind, built by local stonemasons.

7 **Museo Archeologico Regionale Paolo Orsi**
Archaeologist Paolo Orsi gave his name to this museum specializing in artifacts he found in Syracuse *(see pp26–7)*.

8 **Temple of Minerva**
The city's 18th-century Baroque cathedral *(see p47)* incorporates an ancient temple of Minerva, which had been built over the site of a monument to Athena.

10 **Castello Euríalo**
The castle is the most important extant Greek military installation in Sicily. It was built by Dionysus the Younger in the 5th century BC, and improved by Hieron II.

9 **Temple of Apollo**
Dating back to the 6th century BC, this is the oldest Doric temple still standing in western Europe **(above)**. The base has an inscription to the god Apollo.

Museo Archeologico Highlights

Archaeological finds from the necropolis of Pantalica

1 Material from Pantalica
Pantalica, near Palazzolo Acreide, was inhabited by the pre-Greek Sicels, who produced elegant red-glazed pottery.

2 Bronze Age Material from Castelluccio
Materials from the Castelluccio site, between Noto and Palazzolo Acreide, such as bowls, cups and jugs, show trade links between early Sicilians and eastern Mediterranean cultures.

3 Mother Goddess
From the Temple of Megara Hyblaea, this object made of terracotta represents the mother goddess nursing twins. Known in Italian as Madre Dea, she is remarkable for the sense of solidity blended with tenderness.

4 Villa Landolina Gardens
These gardens sit on a site that is rich in finds from locations including an ancient Greek necropolis, parts of Hellenistic streets and Christian catacombs.

5 Greek Kouros, Lentini
This 6th-century-BC *kouros* (statue of a muscular youth) is one of the best examples of ancient Greek sculpture.

6 Gela Vase Collection
A *lekythoi* (tall one-handed vase) painted with *Herakles and the Hydra* is the most impressive.

7 Venus Anadyomene
A Roman copy of a Greek 2nd-century-BC original. From her pose to the high polish of the marble, she is an image of pure sensuality.

8 Ephebus at Adrano
This small athletic bronze figure of an *ephebus* or adolescent was found near Adrano, and dates from around 460 BC.

Museum Floorplan

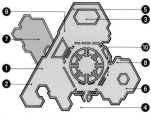

Key to floorplan
▨ Ground floor
▨ First floor

Bronze statue of Ephebus

THE HISTORY OF ANCIENT SYRACUSE

Under the tyrant Gelon, Syracuse formed a mighty alliance with other Greeks at Akragas (Agrigento) and Gela to defeat the Carthaginians at Himera in 480 BC. Hieron I (478–466 BC) and Dionysius (405–367 BC) made Syracuse the most powerful city on the island and in the Mediterranean. In 413 BC Athens sent a fleet in the "Great Expedition" to put down the threat, and with help from Sparta, the Athenians were defeated. Despite their warlord image, Syracuse's rulers were patrons of the arts – Hieron II (265–215 BC) expanded the great theatre and Aeschylus, Pindar, Plutarch and Plato were present at court. After Hieron II's death, however, Syracuse sided not with Rome but with Carthage in the Second Punic War. After a siege lasting two years, Syracuse fell to Rome in 212 BC and began a slow decline.

5th-century bust of a woman made in colourful terracotta.

TOP 10
COLONIES OF ANCIENT SYRACUSE

1 Akrai (Palazzolo Acreide)

2 Kasmenai (Casmene)

3 Kamarina (Camarina)

4 Adronan (Adrano)

5 Thermae (Termini Imerese)

6 Cephaloedium (Cefalù)

7 Katane (Catania)

8 Tauromenium (Taormina)

9 Zancle (Messina)

10 Selinus (Selinunte)

Museo Archeologico Regionale Paolo Orsi has many remnants of the mighty colony of Syracuse, including sculpture and everyday objects.

⑨ Temples of Athena and Apollo

Fragments from two Doric temples on Ortygia are on show, such as polychrome parts of a Gorgon.

⑩ Wooden Statuettes of Demeter and Kore

These rare examples of wooden statuary were found at a sanctuary between Gela and Agrigento. They date from the late 7th century BC and survived because they were covered in the mineral-rich mud of a local spring.

Terracotta relief showing a Gorgon

🔟 ⭐ **Noto**

After the massive earthquake that destroyed almost all of eastern Sicily in 1693, major reconstruction resulted in cities and villages being designed in the Baroque style, then at the height of its popularity. Noto is one of the best examples of the form. Designed specifically to include vistas of the countryside, the urban plan was also sensitive to the needs of the citizens. The soft, locally quarried stone adapted well to the carved decorations, but, unfortunately, the elements have taken their toll on it and renovations have been necessary.

1 **Cattedrale di San Nicolò**
Noto's splendid Baroque cathedral **(above)** sits on top of Labisi's grand staircase. San Nicolò was built in stages throughout the 18th century, with input from architects Gagliardi and Sinatra.

2 **Porta Reale**
The Royal Gate **(left)** was erected in 1838 to greet King Ferdinand II. It offers a grand entrance to Noto's main street, Corso Vittorio Emanuele.

3 **Chiesa di San Francesco**
The 18th-century church of San Francesco has a Baroque portal, stucco interior and a wooden statue of the Virgin Mary.

4 **Chiesa di Montevergini**
An elegantly simple church, with a concave façade, marks the end of Via Nicolaci. Nearby is Palazzo Nicolaci, with its decorated balconies **(above)** supported by carved grotesques.

8 San Carlo al Corso

Built in 1730, the church has various ceiling paintings **(left)** and a graceful concave façade. Wonderfully elegant columns on the façade progress from Doric to Ionic and finally Corinthian. A vertiginous climb to the top of the *campanile* (bell tower) provides beautiful views over the town.

5 Chiesa di San Domenico

Gagliardi's masterpiece (1737) has an exuberant, convex façade, filled with niches and columns creating dramatic contrasts of light and shade.

NEED TO KNOW

MAP G5

Cattedrale di San Nicolò: 9am–1pm & 3–8pm daily

San Carlo al Corso: Corso Vittorio Emanuele; 9am–noon & 3–7pm daily. Adm (bell tower only)

■ Sample Sicilian pastries and *gelati* at Caffè Sicilia, located on the Corso next to San Carlo *(see p80)*.

9 Piazza Municipio, Palazzo Ducezio

The lovely town square is home to the Palazzo Ducezio, now the town hall **(above)**, designed by Sinatra in 1742. A loggia runs along the façade.

6 Palazzi, Via Cavour

Via Cavour is lined with *palazzi* of noble families. The Palazzo Trigona is a stately Baroque design of 1781 with characteristically curved balconies and a frescoed interior. On the corner to the left lies Palazzo Battaglia, which is a late Baroque work by Gagliardi.

10 Old Market, Via Rocco Pirri

Noto's lively market was at one time held in this courtyard, but sadly butchers and bakers have now been replaced by boutiques. However, there is a market with plenty of fresh local produce in town every Monday across from the church of San Domenico.

7 Chiesa di Santa Chiara & Santissimo Salvatore

On opposite sides of the street are the convent of Santa Chiara and the monastery of Santissimo Salvatore. Santa Chiara's oval interior houses a 16th-century *Madonna and Child* sculpted by Sicilian Antonello Gagini.

BAROQUE ARCHITECTURE

The Baroque style grew out of the Renaissance, which used Classical forms and primary shapes to create balance and proportion. Baroque architects applied these forms to curved and ovoid shapes to achieve movement and drama. Typical features include an elliptical floorplan, a façade that projects outward or undulates, the use of light and shade, concave forms, as well as plenty of exuberant decoration.

★ **Villa Romana del Casale**

As the hunting lodge of an important Roman official (perhaps Maximianus, Diocletian's co-emperor), the villa at Piazza Armerina was decorated with what is now the best preserved and most extensive set of Roman mosaics in the world. The lavish villa was constructed over a period of more than 50 years from the late 3rd century to the early 4th century AD, and its airy rooms, peristyles, luxurious thermal baths and gardens with pools and fountains were laid out on four natural terraces.

② **Narthex of the Thermae**
The long narthex in the thermae (gym) is decorated with a circus scene. Horse-drawn chariots career around a track, in the centre of which is an image of the obelisk of Constantinus II.

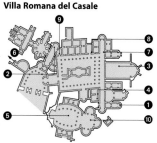

Villa Romana del Casale

① **Arion and Naiads**
The floor of this living room **(above)**, which had marble-faced walls, is decorated with a lively scene of the bejewelled Arion playing a lyre. She is surrounded by naiads.

NEED TO KNOW

MAP F4 ■ Contrada Casale, 6 km (3.5 miles) from Piazza Armerina ■ 093 5680036 ■ www.villaromanadelcasale.it

Open 9am–6pm daily

Adm €10

■ It can get hot inside as most of the villa is housed in a wood and plexiglass structure.

■ In the summer, a courtesy minibus runs from Piazza Armerina.

③ **Private Apartments**
The floors of the family's private apartments **(above)** are decorated with the scenes of a children's hunt. Panels throughout depict foliage, flowers and baskets of fruit and vegetables.

④ **Ten Girls in Bikinis**
Perhaps the most famous mosaic in the villa is the bikini-clad athletes. They appear to have just finished a competition: the winner has been awarded a flower crown and a palm sceptre.

7 Great Hunting Scene

These mosaics show two countries (personified) surrounded by sea. The array of animals on land and in the sea includes lions, elephants, tigers and a leopard attacking a gazelle **(left)**.

10 Triclinium

The triclinium, used for banqueting, opens on one side onto a lovely garden surrounded by an elliptical portico. The mosaics are of a grand scale, in keeping with their subject, the Ten Labours of Hercules.

5 Xystus

On the northern side of the xystus, the elliptical garden off the triclinium, are three rooms decorated with scenes of the *vendemmia* (grape harvest).

6 Aqueduct

Near the entrance to the villa are remains of the aqueduct **(below)**, which provided water for the baths, fountains, gardens and household.

8 Public Room off the Peristyle

The reception room is decorated with a hunting scene **(above)** – one of the earliest mosaics in the villa. Hunters and dogs chase beasts, spear a wild boar and carry it away on their shoulders.

9 Changing Room for the Thermae

Here the emperor's family is shown: his mother, daughter and son, accompanied by their slaves, are carrying equipment they will need for the baths and gym.

MOSAICS

The almost perfectly preserved mosaic floors of the Villa Romana are the result of the house being buried under a mudslide in the 12th century. The mosaic artist (possibly from North Africa) was highly skilled, forming large-scale images from millions of polychrome tiles *(tesserae)* to cover 3,500 sq m (37,670 sq ft) of floor space.

TOP 10 ⭐ Agrigento and the Valle dei Templi

Aligned with Syracuse, Greek Akragas was one of the most important towns in Sicily during the Greek period. It constructed temples to its gods, and was known for breeding horses, with which it consistently won the Olympic Games. After being besieged by the Carthaginians in 406 BC, the town was taken by the Romans in 261 BC, renamed Agrigentum, and remained in Roman control until the fall of the Empire. The ruins of the ancient Greek city are now known as the *Valle dei Templi* (Valley of the Temples).

2 Centro Storico

Pass through the historic centre to get to the Duomo. The route takes visitors from Via Atenea via alleyways and passes artisans' work-shops and local women pausing from their daily chores to chat.

1 Temple of Herakles

Amid olive and almond trees lie the ruins of this hexastyle temple **(above)** dating from around 500 BC. Cross over the ancient street and walk over the stones to see the *cella* wall and Doric columns – beautiful at sunset.

3 San Nicola

The front of the church has an interesting 13th-century portal that reuses materials from a Roman ruin, and a nicely arched interior.

4 Temple of Castor and Pollux

Considered a symbol of Sicily and also known as the Temple of the Dioscuri, this temple **(below)** features four lone columns and entablature that were put together from pieces of other temples in the 19th century.

⑤ Temple of Olympian Zeus

All that remains of this temple is a copy of one of its giant statues **(above)**. The original is in the Archaeological Museum.

Agrigento and the Valle dei Templi

⑥ Temple of Hera

Patches of red at this temple to the queen of the gods (c 450 BC) are fire damage, perhaps from the Carthaginian siege of 406 BC.

⑦ Greek Roads, Gates and Walls

Walking from temple to temple through the valley, visitors can see what is left of the Greek city: rutted roads and city walls bearing the marks from later ages, when gaps were carved into them for new Byzantine tombs and gates.

⑧ Abbazia di Santo Spirito

The resident Cistercian nuns at this 13th-century abbey still practise the old tradition of pastry-making, once the exclusive work of the convents.

⑨ Hellenistic/ Roman Quarter

Among knee-high ruins are door jambs in walls, basins, columns, mills, steps, remains of the drainage system and mosaic flooring.

VALLE DEI TEMPLI GUIDE

The site is divided into three sections, all near a central car park with ticket booth and tourist information office. The Temple of Olympian Zeus and the Sanctuary of the Chthonic Deities are in an area just to the west of the car park. The entrance to the temples along the Via Sacra (Hera, Herakles and Concordia) is across the street. Up the Via dei Templi you will find the Hellenistic/ Roman Quarter and the Museo Archeologico Regionale di Agrigento (see pp34–5).

⑩ Temple of Concordia

The hexastyle Temple of Concordia **(below)** has remained intact because it was converted for use as a church. It dates from 430 BC.

NEED TO KNOW
MAP D4
Valle dei Templi: 092 2621 611; 8:30am–7pm daily (to 10pm in summer, to midnight Sun & public hols). Adm €10
Museo Archeologico Regionale di Agrigento: Contrada S Nicola 12; 092 2401565; 9am– 7:30pm Tue–Sat, 9am– 1:30pm Mon, Sun & hols. Adm €8; combined ticket €13.50; www.parcodei templi.net
San Nicola: Piazza Duomo; open for weddings only

■ Avoid the crowded restaurants at the temple site and have a meal in town (see p123).

■ The temples are spectacular at night, when the buildings are floodlit.

Museo Archeologico Highlights

Archaeological Museum Floorplan

Key to floorplan
- Basement
- Ground floor

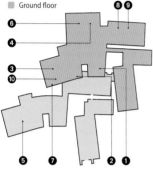

1 Head of a Bull

Materials excavated from both Agrigento and Gela are found in the first two galleries. They include Bronze Age pots painted with red geometric designs, locally produced pottery, as well as Greek finds. One of the most interesting is the little head of a bull, hand-moulded in pinched terracotta.

2 Lion-Head Waterspouts

Recovered from various temples at Agrigento (including the temples of Herakles and Demeter), these spouts, shaped like lions' heads, were originally placed along

the roof of temples, just above the cornice, to funnel rainwater to the ground. Note that they were painted in bright colours, as were all of the elements of the temple above the level of the column capitals.

3 Model of the Temple of Olympian Zeus

This scale reconstruction of the largest known Doric temple in the world, the Temple of Olympian Zeus (see p33), allows visitors to appreciate the once enormous size of the building. Take note of the position of the 8-m- (26-ft-) tall *telamoni* (giant stone figures) in relation to the massive columns. More than twice as tall as these giant figures, the temple's imposing columns measured 16.5 m (54 ft) in height and had a diameter of 4 m (13 ft) at their base.

Marmorean sarcophagus

4 Sarcophagus of a Child

This sarcophagus, dating from the 2nd century BC, was only discovered in the 1970s. The panels, carved in high relief, vividly illustrate scenes from the child's life. There is a detailed scene of the sick room, showing the father pulling his beard in mourning.

5 Roman Quarter Mosaics

These particularly fine Roman mosaics from the 2nd century AD are made of tiny tesserae (tiles). They served as centrepieces to the decorative mosaic flooring of houses in the residential sector of the city.

Display of carved waterspouts

The collection of vases at the Archaeological Museum, Agrigento

6 Vase Collection

The vase collection includes outstanding examples of Attic black-figure and red-figure vases as well as Hellenistic vases. The *krater* (a tall vase with a sturdy base and two handles), with a rare white background, shows the figures of Perseus and Andromeda.

7 Ephebus of Agrigento

Described as an *ephebus* (a youth taking part in a religious rite), this beautifully carved marble figure illustrates the transition from the static archaic style to the severe style. Note the fine modelling of the boy's musculature and the movement of the figure, which dramatically contrasts to the almost Egyptian-like stilted and stiff figures of the former archaic style.

8 Greek and Roman Helmets

Discovered in Eraclea Minoa, the fascinating Greek battle helmets are designed with ear holes, while the Roman ones have a topknot and finely chased rims.

9 Red-figure Krater

The "Battle of the Amazons" (c 460 BC) design on this striking *krater* vase has been attributed to the Niobid painter. The artist skilfully created space on the curved surface by illustrating fallen bodies, bows and arrows, and other battlefield paraphernalia in rough perspective.

The main scene shows Achilles killing an Amazon queen (and falling in love with her as he does so).

10 Telamone and Telamone Heads

Thirty-eight *telamoni* once supported the entablature of the Temple of Olympian Zeus. A complete figure was reconstructed in the 1800s from various parts found on the site. Each of these figures was composed of several stones, covered with a smooth stucco overlay, and probably colour as well. Scholars still debate the exact form and position of the *telamoni*, but it may be that they stood with their feet splayed.

Giant telamone figure

🔟 ⭐ Selinunte

The ruins of ancient Selinunte *(Selinus)*, once a large settlement at the westernmost reaches of Magna Graecia, loom high on a promontory above the sparkling Mediterranean. Now one of the most important archaeological sites in Europe, it boasts one of the largest Greek temples in the world. Selinunte was founded around 608 BC and enjoyed centuries of prosperity before being reduced to rubble by the Carthaginians during the First Punic War.

1 East Group of Temples
Here lie the ruins of three temples **(above)** on which decorative fragments are identifiable. Temple E is an example of balanced Doric order.

2 Temple G
The only octastyle temple at Selinunte (all others are hexastyle), Temple G **(below)** is one of the four largest Greek temples in the world. Its columns are more than 16 m (52 ft) high. It was left unfinished in 480 BC.

3 Temples A and O
Temple A and Temple O, of which only the bases remain, are identical. They were built in Doric style around 480 BC, which makes them the most recent ruins on the Selinunte site.

4 Acropolis
The promontory was levelled by the first settlers, allowing them to build sacred buildings; commercial and residential structures followed.

5 Temple C
Built on a rise, this was the most important temple on the site. It was decorated with polychrome stone and terracotta elements.

6 Fortified Walls of the Acropolis
The original walls, built of large blocks of stone, were reinforced after the city was sacked by Carthage in 409 BC, and a second circle built around 305 BC.

8 Metopes

The metopes **(left)** at Selinunte, carved panels showing scenes from Greek mythology, are now in the Museo Archeologico Regionale Antonio Salinas *(see p92)*. The metopes from temples E and F are outstanding examples of Classical style.

THE ORIENTATION OF SELINUNTE

Selinunte was built on hilltops around the mouths of the Cotone and Selinon (now the Modione) rivers. From the main car park, with the ticket booth, a path leads to the East Group of Temples. The Acropolis is located across the valley (the location of the old harbour) and is accessible on foot or by car; the site's second car park is located at its base. The sanctuary of Malophorus, reached by walking west from the Acropolis, cannot be accessed by private cars.

9 North Gate

Of great importance for the defence of Selinunte, the 7-m- (23-ft-) high North Gate was protected by a sophisticated fortification composed of three bastions and a double line of walls. After sustaining damage in 409 BC, the earlier ring of walls was reinforced.

10 Sanctuary of Malophorus

This funerary sanctuary **(left)** is dedicated to Malophorus, who was the pomegranate-bearing goddess. The elegant piece was in use from the 7th to the 3rd centuries BC.

Selinunte

EAST GROUP

ACROPOLIS

MARINELLA

400 metres

7 Commercial Area and Stoa

Behind Temple D you can see the remains of shops, each with two rooms, a courtyard and stairs that led to the shopkeepers' apartments on the upper floors.

NEED TO KNOW

MAP B4 ■ Marinella di Selinunte, SS 115 south of Castelvetrano ■ 092 446277

Open 9am–6pm (to 4pm in winter); visitors should ensure that they have purchased tickets by 4pm) Adm €6

■ There is a stunning view of the ruins from the sea off Marinella beach.

■ The tourist office at Castelvetrano organizes site tours in golf carts.

■ Have a picnic dinner amid the ruins while enjoying dance or music. Details at the ticket booth.

Features of a Doric Temple

1 Proportion
Greek architecture followed rules of proportion to ensure the beauty and harmony of the finished structure. Doric temples were built with a length-to-width ratio of 3:1 or 2:1. Column height was related proportionally to base diameter, with columns gradually becoming more slender over the centuries.

2 Columns
Doric columns have a simple capital and a fluted shaft without a base. The shaft is larger in diameter at the bottom than at the top.

Fluted Doric columns

3 Colonnade
When columns are arranged around the outer edge of a temple's *crepidoma* (base), they form a colonnade. "Peripteral" refers to a single colonnade and "dipteral" to a double colonnade.

4 Pediments
The triangular gables above the entablature on a temple's short sides are the pediments, usually decorated with figures or reliefs.

Entablature and column

5th-century BC altar at Temple A

5 Altar
A carved block of stone used for animal sacrifices was placed outside temples at the eastern end.

6 Frieze
This is the decorative feature of the entablature. It is made up of alternating triglyphs – grooved blocks ending in little teeth *(guttae)* – which support the structure above and metopes (broad panels usually carved with figurative scenes).

7 Roof
Roofs were made of wooden beams and terracotta tiles. They frequently had polychrome decorations such as gargoyles cast into the shapes of animals' heads, which functioned as waterspouts.

8 Colour
The architectural elements and sculpted pieces, particularly the parts of the entablature and the pediment, were always painted in bright colours (polychrome) – most typically in red, blue, white or yellow.

9 Cella
Each temple housed a sanctuary *(cella)*, usually an enclosed room in the centre of the temple. Here the sacred image or statue of a god or goddess was kept.

10 Entablature
The entablature rests above the capitals and below the pediment.

THE RISE AND FALL OF SELINUS

Selinus, which was named after the abundant wild celery *(selinon)* which still grows in the area, enjoyed prosperity and power with a sprawling urban complex of 80,000 inhabitants, impressive temple compounds, their own mint and extensive agricultural holdings. Located on the edge of Greek territory, Selinus was forced to fight border wars with Segesta and was in constant danger from attack by their mighty Carthaginian allies. Although it gradually accepted some Carthaginian influence and even declared itself neutral in the Battle of Himera (480 BC) between the warring Carthaginians and Syracusan Greeks, it preferred to remain a Greek ally. Selinus lost that right in 409 BC, when Hannibal and his forces sacked the town, forcing all inhabitants to abandon the residential sector. From then until its demise, Selinus was restricted to the refortified Acropolis and remained under Punic control. Selinus was finally abandoned in 250 BC, when Carthage, fighting Rome during the First Punic War, moved all residents to its stronghold at Lilybaeum (modern-day Marsala). A small community was located at Selinus during the Christian era, but it too was eventually abandoned and all knowledge of the town, even its name, was lost until archaeologists uncovered it in the 19th century.

Gelon's triumphal entry into Syracuse is shown in this painting by Giuseppe Carta (1853). Gelon, king of Syracuse, saw off the Carthaginians at the Battle of Himera (480 BC).

TOP 10
FINDS FROM SELINUNTE

1 Punishment of Acteon (470 BC)

2 Efebo (bronze statue, 470 BC)

3 Zeus and Hera (470 BC)

4 Perseus and the Gorgon (c 560–550 BC)

5 Statue of a Kore (6th century BC)

6 Tumminìa Wheat

7 Europa and the Bull (6th century BC)

8 Corinthian Oinochoe (6th century BC)

9 Attic Lekane (6th century BC)

10 Bronze Zeus (6th century BC)

Metope depicting Perseus beheading Medusa

The Top 10 of Everything

**Christ Pantocrator,
Monreale Cathedral**

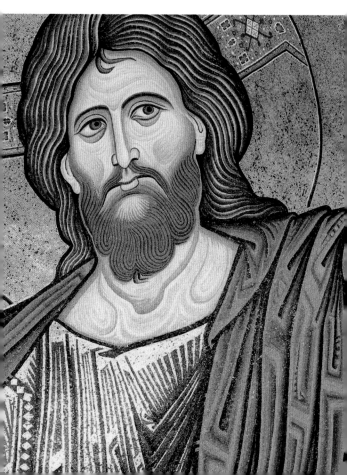

Moments in History

❶ Ducetius

Ducetius unified his people, the Sicels of eastern Sicily, against the Greeks in 452 BC. He succeeded in fortifying positions and redistributing land until suffering final defeat at the hands of Syracuse.

❷ Supremacy of Syracuse

The Syracusan tyrants Hieron I, Gelon and Dionysus I assured the ascendancy of Greek Sicily, with Syracuse at the helm. The Greek colonies fought among themselves, but united when it was necessary, including to defeat the Carthaginians at Himera in 480 BC.

❸ Roman Rule

Rome's successful siege of Syracuse in 212 BC marked the end of Greek power on the island. After centuries of warfare, Roman rule brought peace. *Praetors* were sent to Sicily to govern, including Verres, later prosecuted by Cicero for his misdeeds. Verres was the first in a long line of foreign plunderers.

Silver coin depicting winged victory

❹ Arab Invasion

After Byzantine rule for three centuries, the North African Moors invaded in AD 827 at Mazara del Vallo. They captured Palermo, made it their capital and turned it into the cosmopolitan city it remains today. They improved rural infrastructure and irrigation, and introduced new methods of agriculture and fishing.

❺ Count Roger

Norman crusader Roger de Hauteville (also known as Count Roger or Roger I) took Sicily between 1061 and 1091. He was the first of a century of Norman rulers who slowly changed Sicily from an eastern to a western society, albeit one with exotic flair *(see p13)*.

❻ The Sicilian Vespers

After decades of rule by the French Angevins, in 1282 an uprising began in Palermo. Having successfully instigated revolt and done away with the unpopular foreign sovereign, Sicilians invited Peter of Aragón to become their king.

Norman fleet of Roger de Hauteville in the 11th century

7 Unification

Centuries of misrule, foreign domination and the feudal system meant wealth, power and land fell into the hands of the few. Popular revolts began in 1820, reached a head in 1848, and in May 1860 the Italian socialist Garibaldi, with the aid of Sicilian Redshirts, took the island and convinced the peasant class to vote for Italian Unification.

Garibaldi leads the expedition

8 Emigration

After Unification, however, Sicily found itself highly taxed and ignored as an outpost of a "foreign" government. Peasant farmers were unable to feed their families and there was no sign of improvement. Such poverty was behind the mass emigration to the Americas in the late 1800s and early 1900s.

9 Earthquakes

In 1908 an earthquake killed over 70,000 people and levelled more than 90 per cent of Messina. Another damaging quake, in 1968, left scores of villages destroyed in the Belice valley. Thousands were housed in shelters for 15 years, waiting for the government to resolve the problem.

10 Mafia Crackdown

The conviction of 350 *mafiosi* during the 1980s led to the murder of the judges Giovanni Falcone and Paolo Borsellino in 1992. "Boss of Bosses" Salvatore "Totò" Riina was convicted of arranging the murders.

TOP 10 MYTHOLOGICAL FIGURES

1 Aeneas
Aeneas fled Troy, found refuge on Sicily, and founded Erice and Segesta.

2 Demeter
Goddess of agriculture, the harvest and fertility. Her cult was based at Enna.

3 Persephone
Demeter's daughter was taken by Hades into the underworld at Lake Pergusa.

4 Hephaestus (Vulcan)
The god of fire lived on Mount Etna, forging his father Zeus's lightning bolts with the flames of the volcano.

5 Odysseus (Ulysses)
The Greek military leader wandered the Mediterranean for 10 years trying to get home. Many of his adventures took place on Sicily.

6 Polyphemus
The giant one-eyed Cyclops shepherd and cannibal held Odysseus hostage in his Mount Etna cave.

7 Aeolios
The King of the Winds and master of navigation lived on the Aeolian Islands.

8 Arethusa
Chased by the river god Alpheus, Arethusa threw herself into the Ionian Sea and sprung up at Syracuse, transformed into a fountain.

9 Acis
Murdered by the jealous Polyphemus, Acis was reincarnated as a river and gave his name to nine towns on the Ionian coast.

10 Scylla and Charybdis
These hideous sea monsters dwelled on either side of the Straits of Messina, terrorizing passing sailors.

Relief of deities and their horses

🔟 Ancient Sites

1 Syracuse

The Greeks founded a colony here in 733 BC and began a project of development and expansion that led to Syracuse becoming the most powerful city in the Mediterranean. Remains of defensive structures and sacred, social and residential areas are visible today. A comprehensive archaeology museum makes sense of the varied ruins (see pp24–7).

2 Solunto

This small village was under Carthaginian control, along with Motya and Palermo, until it was taken by the Romans around 250 BC. The urban grid pattern clearly remains and the paved streets are lined with residences and shops, some with traces of ancient wall decoration, mosaics, columns and cisterns. The latter were of supreme importance because Solunto's position on a promontory above the Tyrrhenian Sea did not offer any natural water sources (see p102).

3 Taormina

Sited in a spectacular position on Monte Tauro, the 3rd-century-BC Greek theatre at Taormina is the second largest in Sicily, but ranks first for the beauty of its backdrop. The view of Reggio di Calabria, the Ionian Sea and Mount Etna is broken only by the *scena* – marble-faced niches and columns added later by the Romans (see pp18–19).

Greek theatre with its stunning backdrop, Taormina

Remains of a Greek temple, Selinunte

4 Selinunte

The archaeological park here protects the ruins of eight massive temples, including one of the largest known temples of the ancient world, Temple C. There are also visible remains of Phoenician, Greek, Carthaginian and Byzantine settlements (see pp36–9).

5 Morgantina

Morgantina was an important commercial centre along the trade route from the north coast of Sicily and the Aeolian Islands to the south. Deep in Sicani and Sicel territory, the city flourished during the Hellenistic and Roman periods, and extensive ruins date from that time (see p117).

6 Segesta

This peaceful and beautiful site comprises the ruins of one of the most important cities of the Elimi, the Hellenized Sicani peoples, and one of the most perfect Doric temples ever constructed. The temple's purpose is unknown, adding mystery to the already ethereal site (see p100).

7 Agrigento

In the grounds of the Valle dei Templi lie Greek temples, and a sanctuary to the goddesses Demeter and Persephone, the so-called Rock Sanctuary. The medieval centre of the town is almost buried by modern development, though fascinating pieces of Greek structures were incorporated into it *(see pp32–5)*.

8 Villa Romana del Casale

The remains of a luxury hunting villa for a Roman official hold the best extant Roman mosaic cycle in the world. The rich figurative and decorative designs adorn the floors of the villa *(see pp30–31)*.

Mosaic at the Villa Romana del Casale

9 Motya

The island city in the lagoon between Marsala and Trapani was used from the 8th century BC by the Phoenicians to control shipping routes in the eastern Mediterranean. It became a Carthaginian stronghold until its destruction by Syracuse in 398 BC. Today, walls with fortified gates and towers surround the entire perimeter and there is a man-made harbour within the walls. Ancient paved roads, sacred and residential areas can also be seen *(see p101)*.

10 Tindari

The ruins of ancient Tyndaris are remarkably well preserved. This was one of the last Greek colonies in Sicily, founded by the Syracusans in 396 BC. Features include the remains of a Roman villa and baths, and an amphitheatre *(see p111)*.

TOP 10 ARCHITECTURAL STYLES

Palazzo dei Normanni, Palermo

1 Phoenician
The Phoenician rectangular block walls fortified the ancient cities of Erice and Motya and built the foundations of the Palazzo dei Normanni.

2 Greek
Doric temples and semicircular theatres are what remain from the years Sicily spent under Greek rule.

3 Roman
Aqueducts and lavish patrician homes embellished with mosaics are the most common examples of this style.

4 Arab Norman
The golden age of Sicily saw the blending of sharp northern arches and arabesque red-coloured domes.

5 Spanish Baroque
The arrival of the Jesuits brought intricate marble inlays (intarsia) adorning church walls and altars.

6 Late Sicilian Baroque
An innovation created after the 1693 earthquake, this style can be seen in sandstone *palazzi* with grand stairways and intricate embellishments.

7 Neo Classical
Greco-Roman revival style featuring frescoes with colours from Pompeii ruins.

8 Neo Gothic
The gilded façade of the Palazzo dei Normanni is a prime example of this 18th-century movement.

9 Art Nouveau
The exquisite floral arts movement was the inspiration behind the ornate Villa Igiea in Palermo.

10 Ventennio
Austere white buildings such as the central post office or the courthouse in Palermo remain from the Fascist era.

🔟 Places of Worship

Palermo's Byzantine masterpiece, La Martorana

1 La Martorana and San Cataldo, Palermo

Excellent examples of Arab-Norman architecture. The former has the only known portrait of King Roger II (see p91). San Cataldo has its original unadorned exterior and interior.

2 San Domenico, Palermo

Sicily's most illustrious citizens are buried here, including physicist Stanislao Cannizzaro and painter Pietro Novelli (see p91).

San Domenico church, Palermo

3 Monreale

The monastery and cathedral of Santa Maria La Nova were founded by William II in 1174. His tomb, along with the tombs of his father, King William I, and mother, Queen Margaret, are in the south transept (see pp14–15).

4 San Carlo al Corso, Noto

Dedicated to San Carlo Borromeo, this 18th-century church is located on the Corso and forms part of Noto's dramatic Baroque skyline. Climb the tower, which houses three bells, for views of the town's historical centre (see p29).

5 Other Faiths, Palermo

Mosque: MAP L4; Piazza Gran Cancelliere 6; opening times vary ▪ Evangelical Church: MAP D2; Via Parlatore Giuseppe 12; opening times vary ▪ Anglican Church: MAP L2; Via Mariano Stabile 118; opening times vary

Given its long history of invasion (see pp52–3), Sicily has always been a cosmopolitan island, particularly in its capital. Palermo is home to places of worship for a number of faiths and includes a mosque – a reminder of its former Arab inhabitants.

6 Cappella Palatina, Palermo

This masterpiece of Arab-Norman art celebrates both the Glory of God and Norman rule. Masses are said in the richly decorated chapel (see p13).

7 San Giorgio, Ragusa

MAP F5 ▪ Piazza Duomo
▪ Open 9:30am–noon, 4–7pm daily

The cathedral of Ragusa Ibla is built on a rise in a wide tree-lined piazza in the old town. The undulating façade is typical of the architect Gagliardi, supporting a central tower, bulging columns and swirly volutes.

8 Cathedral, Syracuse

MAP H5 ▪ Piazza Duomo
▪ Open 7:30am–8pm daily ▪ Adm

This site of a Catholic place of worship is unique for being set within a previous sacred site. Behind the Baroque façade, the structure of a Greek temple to Minerva has been adapted for use as a church.

9 San Nicola, Agrigento

This 13th-century church is found within the Valle dei Templi. Taking on a majestic golden hue at sunset, its façade mixes Gothic motifs with ancient Roman columns. In a chapel on the right, there is a Roman sarcophagus with reliefs of Greek mythology (see p32).

Byzantine interior, Cefalù Cathedral

10 Cathedral, Cefalù

MAP E2 ▪ Piazza Duomo
▪ 092 1922021 ▪ Ring for admittance (opening times change monthly)
▪ Adm to cloisters

In 1131, after a stormy crossing, Norman King Roger II landed at Cefalù and, giving thanks to God, commissioned the cathedral now famous for its Byzantine mosaic decoration and its restored cloisters. The church has two typically Norman square bell towers (see p110).

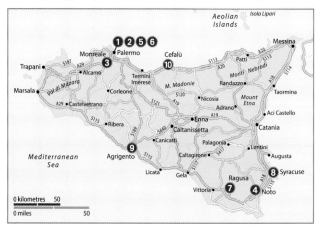

🔟 Castles

Impregnable walls of Castello Ursino

1 Castello Ursino, Catania
MAP G4 ■ Piazza Federico di Svevia ■ Open 9am–7pm daily (last entry 6:30pm) ■ Adm

Built around 1250, the once-moated castle has been used variously as a royal residence, the seat of parliament and a prison. It now houses the town's Museo Civico.

2 Castello di Lombardia, Enna
MAP E4 ■ Open 8am–8pm daily

One of the largest castles in Sicily was built by Frederick II in 1233 on this high point. Massive walls and six towers remain. The octagonal Torre di Federico II is the only fully original part standing.

3 Castello Ventimiglia, Castelbuono
MAP E3 ■ Open 9:30am–1pm, 3:30–7pm daily ■ Adm

In 1316 the Ventimiglia family built their fortified family seat on top of a rocky outcrop in the Madonie mountains. Within is a Baroque chapel dedicated to Sant'Anna by Giacomo Serpotta (1652–1732).

4 Aci Castello
MAP G4 ■ Open 9am–1pm, 3:30–7pm daily (to 5pm winter) ■ Adm

The castle is perched atop a black promontory, jutting out over the sea. Built by the Normans, it was covered by lava flows in 1169. It was rebuilt, then partially destroyed by Frederick II of Aragón in 1297. A stairway scales the side of the fortifications, giving access to the interior. The passages and chambers hold the archaeological collection of the Museo Civico.

5 Caccamo
MAP D3 ■ Open 9am–1pm, 3–7pm Tue–Sun ■ Adm

This 12th-century Norman castle dominates the village and valley below. Pass through the mighty walls, walk among ramparts and visit the *Sala di Congiura* (Hall of the Conspiracy), where in 1160 barons plotted to overthrow King William I.

Caccamo castle and the village below

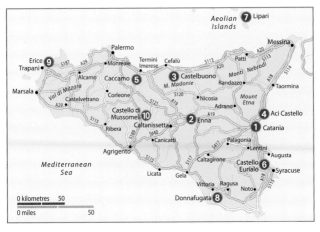

6 Castello Eurialo

These 5th-century-BC fortifications protected the western access to Greek Syracuse. Archimedes added a drawbridge, trenches and catapults to protect the keep, entered through tunnels from the trench (see p128).

7 Castello, Lipari

MAP G1 ■ Open 9am–6:30pm Mon–Sat, 9am–1:30pm Sun & public hols

Lipari's castle rock has been fortified for six millennia. The 12th-century Norman gate offers a passage through walls fortified by the Greeks in the 4th century BC and again by the Spanish in 1556.

8 Castello di Donnafugata

MAP F6 ■ Open 9am–12:30pm daily & 2:45–5:45pm Tue, Sat & Sun ■ Adm

Donnafugata is a mix of architectural styles. The Arabs fortified the site around AD 1000; it then became a castle around 1300. In 1865 a Venetian Gothic loggia was added.

9 Castello di Venere, Erice

MAP B2 ■ Via Conte Pepoli ■ Open Apr, May & Oct: 10am–6pm daily; Jul & Sep: 10am–7pm daily; Aug: 10am–8pm daily (last entry 7:30pm) ■ Adm

This Norman castle is impressively sited on a sheer cliff face. Inside, the remains of Norman walls surround the ancient area sacred to Venus Erycina – stones from her temple were used to build the castle. There are also Phoenician and Roman ruins here.

Vertiginous site of Castello di Venere

10 Castello di Mussomeli

MAP E4 ■ Caltanissetta, Messina ■ Open 9am–noon & 3–6pm Tue–Sun (winter: 9am–noon) ■ Adm

Built on an 80-m- (262-ft-) high limestone rock, this castle is a fine example of 14th-century Gothic architecture. It is considered to be nearly impenetrable due to the sheer drops and its thick crannied walls.

🔟 Museums

Reliefs in the Museo Archeologico Regionale Antonio Salinas, Palermo

① Museo Archeologico Regionale Antonio Salinas, Palermo

Housed in a former palace, this museum is dedicated to the famous archaeologist Antonio Salinas. The objects on display here were recovered from sites in western Sicily and show the development of art and culture from prehistoric eras to the Roman period *(see p92)*.

② Galleria Regionale di Sicilia, Palazzo Abatellis, Palermo

The Catalan-Gothic palace was built at the end of the 15th century and is now home to the collections of the former National Museum. Paintings and sculpture by Sicilian masters

The Triumph of Death, **Palazzo Abatellis**

span the 13th to 16th centuries, complemented by fine works by Italian and Flemish artists *(see p91)*.

③ Museo Archeologico Regionale Paolo Orsi, Syracuse

This is one of the most important archaeological museums in Sicily and documents the ancient cultures and civilizations of both Syracuse and eastern Sicily *(see pp26–7)*.

④ Museo Mandralisca, Cefalù

MAP E2 ▪ Via Mandralisca 13 ▪ 092 1421547 ▪ Open 9am–7pm daily ▪ Adm ▪ www.fondazione mandralisca.it

The museum contains great archaeological finds, including ancient Greek and Arab vases, and an art gallery with works by Sicilian artists. Antonello da Messina's *Portrait of a Man* (1465) is here.

⑤ Museo Regionale di Messina

MAP H2 ▪ Viale della Libertà 465, Messina ▪ 090 361292 ▪ Open 9am–1:30pm daily, 4–6:30pm Tue, Thu, Sat ▪ Adm

This museum is home to some architectural, sculptural and decor-ative fragments recovered from churches after the 1908 earthquake, as well as paintings and sculpture, including two works by Caravaggio.

6 Museo del Sale, Paceco

Housed in a restored windmill, exhibits here trace each stage of traditional salt-making, from filling the saltpans with seawater, to evaporation, recovering, cleaning, storing and grinding the salt (see p66).

7 Museo Archeologico Regionale Eoliano, Lipari

Objects on display in this interesting museum range from obsidian tools of the Neolithic period to items acquired through foreign trade, such as Etruscan red-glazed ceramics. There are also beautiful vases and masks from Greece that have survived from Sicily's Greek occupation (see p17).

8 Le Ciminiere, Catania

MAP G4 ■ Viale Africa ■ 095 4011928 ■ Museo dello Sbarco: open Jun–Aug: 10am–5pm Tue–Sun; Sep–May: 9am–4pm; guided tour only ■ Adm

Literally "the chimneys", this former sulphur works is now a lively cultural centre. Features include the Museo dello Sbarco, a moving reminder of the US and British landings in Sicily in 1943, a cinema museum (see p66) and a traditional puppet theatre.

Traditional Sicilian puppets

9 Casa-Museo di Antonino Uccello, Palazzolo Acreide

The mission of Antonino Uccello was to preserve what he saw as the fast-disappearing culture of peasant farmers and the range of traditional handmade items they used. Exhibits include puppets, decorated carts, the living quarters of a peasant home and elegantly crafted tools, illustrating a unique aspect of Sicilian history (see p129).

Stone head, Agrigento's archaeological museum

10 Museo Archeologico Regionale di Agrigento

Archaeological finds from Agrigento and related cities reveal the Bronze Age, Hellenization and the Roman era (see pp34–5).

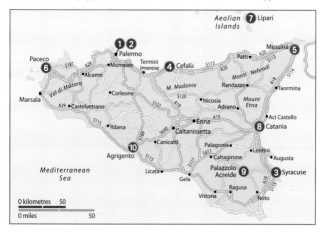

🔟 Vestiges of Invading Powers

Aqueduct across the valley

la pettina (the comb) in Syracuse is left over from the Greeks. The tiny, winding streets of Palermo's old neighbourhoods such as La Kalsa, or the street plan of Castelvetrano, come from Arab settlements. Cefalù's system of parallel streets leading down to the sea is Norman.

① Waterworks
The Greeks and Romans used aqueducts and water-powered mills, while the Arabs introduced land irrigation to the area.

② Dialect
The 22 dialects around the island are a testament to the great overlapping of cultures over the centuries. Words still in use include *naca* (crib) from Greek, *giuggilena* (sesame) from Arabic and *travagliare* (to work) from French. In the town of Piana degli Albanesi, the locals speak Arbëresh, derived from 16th-century Albanian.

③ Place Names
Many place names are Italian versions of original Greek or Latin names. Erice was known as Monte San Giuliano until Mussolini went on a name-changing spree and adopted an Italian version of its original Greek name, Eryx. Arabic names remain in abundance – look for names with the prefixes "Calta", "Gibil" and "Sala".

④ Urban Plans
Modern towns often follow ancient street patterns. The area of narrow straight streets known as

⑤ Farming Techniques
The Arabs systematically farmed according to plant type, bringing about more flavourful and bountiful harvests – especially of olives, which yielded a better olive oil. Irrigated by the *gebbia*, a nearby water cistern, they also knew when to stop the water supply to citrus fruits to get a richer flavour.

Penne all'arrabbiata

⑥ Pasta
Fresh pasta, made of regular wheat flour, was produced in Italy as early as the Etruscan era. Dried pasta, which can be stored, was probably invented by the Arabs using Sicily's *semola*, a hard durum wheat flour.

⑦ Crops
The Spanish introduced tomatoes, potatoes, chocolate and the prickly pear cactus, or *fico d'India*; the Greeks brought olive trees and grapevines; the Arabs citrus fruits, sugar cane, date palms, pistachios, flax, cotton and mulberries.

Fishing Techniques

Sicily's now famous fishing techniques were adapted from Arabic methods. Tuna fishermen still practise the *mattanza* in the channel between Levanzo and Favignana, encouraging tuna through a system of nets to the final "chamber of death", where they are brought close to the surface to be killed. Fishermen work together chanting rhythmically to haul them aboard and to shore. Near Messina, swordfish are spotted from a tall mast and harpooned using a boat called a *feluche*.

Traditional swordfish harpooning

Erosion

The Romans began the deforestation of the island to export timber and make way for wheat plantations. Sicily now has few trees and the earth is washed away in heavy rains.

Fortified Towers

The Spanish protected Sicily's coastline by constructing more than 100 defensive towers. Messages were passed by fire signals.

Fortified towers along Scopello coast

TOP 10 INVADERS

Battle of Himera, Punic Wars

1 Greeks
The first Greek colony founded at Naxos in 734 BC displaced Sicel inhabitants.

2 Carthaginians
Carthage invaded repeatedly and many Punic War battles were fought on Sicily.

3 Romans
After years of warfare, Rome finally took Sicily following the fall of Syracuse back in 212 BC.

4 Byzantines
In AD 535 Sicily became part of Justinian's Eastern Roman Empire.

5 Arabs
The Arab conquest of the island began in AD 827 and was complete only in AD 902 with the fall of Taormina.

6 Normans
After 30 years of crusades, Count Roger de Hauteville finally took Sicily in 1091 (see p42).

7 Spaniards
Peter of Aragón was crowned King of Sicily in 1282, beginning nearly 440 years of Spanish domination.

8 Bourbons
Sicily was given to the House of Savoy in the 1713 Peace of Utrecht treaty, and swapped for Sardinia seven years later, thereby coming under Habsburg rule.

9 Italians
Garibaldi and his Redshirts invaded at Marsala in 1860, starting the campaign that ended with the Unification of Italy.

10 Allied Forces
On 10 July 1943, Allied Forces under generals Patton and Montgomery landed at Licata and Pachino, taking Sicily in 38 days (see p51, Le Ciminiere).

Customs and Traditions

1 Hand Gestures

A Grand Tour author reported that Sicilians had been using hand gestures since the Greek invasion as a way of furthering resistance against foreign rule. Some of the common gestures you see mean: "She's pretty," "This tastes great," "Let's go," "I couldn't care less," "Do you want to stop for a coffee?", "Be careful," "That's not such a good idea," and even "His wife is cheating on him."

2 The Sicilian Cart

Once used for transport, these wooden carts are painted in bright colours and depict scenes from traditional Sicilian puppet shows. They often feature in local parades.

Decorated Sicilian cart

3 Festivals

Festivals for patron saints once offered the only chance for a holiday, and entertainment. Feasts were often in spring, giving farmers a chance to rest after the planting and to pray for a successful harvest. The *festa* was the one day everyone came in from the fields for religious processions, games, horse races, music and fireworks (see pp86–7).

Sicilian *botte* full of bottles of wine

4 Wine

A glass of new wine is enjoyed with *i muffuletti* (round sandwich bread baked with fennel seeds and dressed with salt and oil) on St Martin's Day – usually strong, amber-coloured wine retrieved from the *botte* (barrel). Many families have at least enough grapevines for a yearly *botte* of wine, keeping it in the cellar, in the garage or any other cool spot they can find.

5 Proverbs

Sicilians always have a quip spoken in dialect. Examples include: *Cu' avi 'nna bona vigna, avi pani, vinu e ligna* (He who owns a good vineyard has bread, wine and wood); *Cu nun 'sapi l'arti, chiudi putia* (He who does not know his craft, closes his shop); *Soggira e nora calaru di n'celu sciarriannu*s (Mothers-in-law and daughters-in-law were sent from heaven and started fighting before they hit the ground); and *La soggira voli bene a la nora comu n'rizzu n'pettu* (Mothers-in-law love their daughters-in-law like a sea urchin in the bed).

6 Legends

King Roger's 12th-century French court poets told stories of Charlemagne and the paladins and the King Arthur cycle, which once included Sicily in its milieu. The paladins survive today as puppet theatre heroes (see pp68–9).

7 I Morti

All Souls Day on 2 November is a major celebration. Families visit the cemetery, where tombs have been rigorously tidied up and adorned with fresh flowers for the glory of the dead and for the approval of family members and anyone else passing. Relatives from the other world (or this world) leave children gifts, such as toys, *frutta martorana* (fake fruits crafted from almond paste) and *pupi di cera*, garishly coloured sugar dolls.

8 Olive Oil

On 11 November – St Martin's Day – families celebrate their new, thick, spicy, green olive oil by trying it on *i muffuletti*. If they don't have their own olive trees, families obtain a year's supply of olive oil from a relative or another trusted source, making sure to have a full *giara*, a waist-high terracotta storage jar.

9 La Befana

This craggy old woman who declined an invitation to join the Three Kings bringing gifts to Christ in the manger regretted her decision, set out on her own, and has been travelling the earth ever since with a large sackful of gifts. At Epiphany (6 January) she fills children's socks with presents if they've been good, or with coal (usually of the sweet, edible kind) if they've been bad.

10 Artisanal Fishing

Fishing is big business, but there are still artisanal fleets fishing using colourful nets, homemade lobster pots and *cannizzi*, handmade cane switches for aggravating the fish.

Repairing nets after a day's fishing

TOP 10 SMALL-TOWN TRADITIONS

Playing cards in the sun

1 Old men sitting outside
Old men often sit on a park bench to chat. They may go home for lunch and return to their spot in the afternoon.

2 Naming babies
The first-born child is named after the paternal grandparents, the second child after the maternal ones.

3 Weddings
Weddings can be whole-town affairs, where bride- and groom-to-be open their future home to well-wishers.

4 Folk groups
Folk groups, as keepers of the ancient traditions, perform in period costumes and sing in dialect.

5 Patron saints
Townspeople celebrate and give thanks to their patron saint with a multiday feast and procession through the town.

6 Good Friday
The biggest religious event of the year. Everyone dresses up and follows the procession through the streets.

7 Easter Monday
The unofficial start of the summer, when everyone retreats to the countryside for an all-day barbecue.

8 Wearing black
In small towns people can wear black for years after the death of a loved one.

9 Sitting outdoors in summer
Even people without a garden will often sit outside in summer. You can see them on portable chairs talking or watching (a portable) TV.

10 Buying from a travelling vendor
Fruit and vegetable vendors sell produce from the back of their truck. Shoppers will lower a basket from their balcony to make a purchase.

Artists, Writers and Composers

Late 19th-century illustration of the Greek tragedy *Prometheus Bound*

1 Aeschylus

The "father of Greek tragedy" (525–456 BC) was born near Athens but made extended visits to Sicily. Only seven of around 500 plays have survived, among them *Agamemnon*, *Oedipus* and *Prometheus Bound*. Many of his plays were premiered in Syracuse's theatre *(see p25)*, where they are still performed.

2 Antonello da Messina

The Messina-born Antonello (c 1430–79) is one of the masters of Italian Renaissance art. He is known for detail, intriguing portraits and the luminous quality of his paintings achieved through his skilful use of oil paints, learned from the Flemish masters. Italian Renaissance artists adopted oils in his wake, making it the standard medium for the world's greatest masterpieces. Antonello works remain in museums in Cefalù, Palermo, Messina and Syracuse.

3 The Gagini Family

Domenico Gagini (d 1492) and his son Antonello (1478–1536) set the style for architecture and sculpture in Sicily during the 15th and 16th centuries. The Gagini combined Renaissance and Gothic forms to create uniquely Sicilian pieces.

4 Giacomo Serpotta

Born in Palermo, Serpotta (1656–1732) decorated Baroque interiors, creating an aesthetic transition between architecture and painting by covering the area with figures and scenes modelled in stucco.

Portrait of Vincenzo Bellini

5 Vincenzo Bellini

The composer (1801–35) was born in Catania, trained in Naples and is buried in Catania's cathedral. His successful early works led to commissions for La Scala in Milan. *The Sleepwalker* and *Norma* are among his most successful operas.

6 Luigi Pirandello

 Born at Caos near Agrigento, Pirandello (1867–1936) is known as the founder of 20th-century drama with plays such as *Six Characters in Search of an Author* (1921).

7 Giuseppe Tomasi di Lampedusa

Lampedusa (1896–1957) is the author of *Il Gattopardo (The Leopard)*, a portrait of Sicilian aristocracy pre- and post-Unification. It was based on the life of his great-grandfather and published posthumously.

8 Salvatore Quasimodo

Born in Modica, novelist and poet Quasimodo (1901–68) wrote anti-Fascist works in a political climate that made it necessary to disguise his message. He was awarded the Nobel Prize in 1959.

9 Renato Guttuso

Originally from Bagheria, Guttuso (1912–87) painted energetic Expressionistic canvases that illustrated Sicilian peasant life and spoke out against the Mafia and Fascism.

10 Leonardo Sciascia

Sciascia (1921–89) was a political essayist and novelist. Works such as *The Wine Dark Sea* give an insight into the complicated world of Sicilian thinking and Mafia culture.

Novelist Leonardo Sciascia

Burt Lancaster in *Il Gattopardo*

TOP 10 FILMS SET IN SICILY

1 Il Gattopardo
Luchino Visconti's 1963 film version of Lampedusa's novel stars Burt Lancaster.

2 Divorzio all'Italiana
Marcello Mastroianni is a Sicilian aristocrat seeking a divorce in Pietro Germi's 1961 comedy.

3 A Ciascuno il Suo
Adapted from a Sciascia novel, a look into the Mafia and life in 1960s Sicily, directed by Elio Petri in 1967.

4 La Terra Trema
Visconti's 1948 adaptation of Verga's *I Malavoglia*, the story of a fisherman's failed dream of independence.

5 The Godfather (*Il Padrino*)
Francis Ford Coppola's iconic Mafia saga was based on the book by Mario Puzo.

6 Cento Giorni a Palermo
Giuseppe Ferrara's 1983 film tells the story of policeman Carlo Alberto Dalla Chiesa, murdered by the Mafia after just 100 days on the job.

7 Kaos
A 1984 film adaptation of four Pirandello stories.

8 Cinema Paradiso
Giuseppe Tornatore's 1989 Academy Award-winning film takes a romantic look at growing up in a remote village.

9 Il Postino
Shot on Salina, this film is about a Sicilian postman whose life is turned around through his friendship with the Chilean poet Pablo Neruda (1994).

10 I Cento Passi
Marco Tullio Giordana recounts the life of anti-Mafia activist Peppino Impastato in this 2002 film.

⏫ Villages

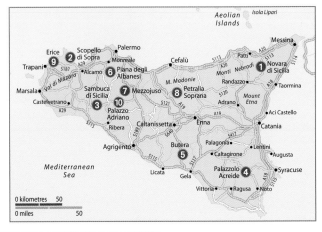

In the mountains, Novara di Sicilia

1 Novara di Sicilia
MAP G2

This little mountain village is tucked between the Peloritani and Nebrodi mountain ranges. The medieval site has a crumbling Arab castle and the 16th-century Chiesa Madre with naive wood carvings on the altar.

2 Scopello di Sopra
MAP C2

This small village of fishermen was almost inaccessible until the road was built from Castellammare. Now the village is experiencing something of a tourist boom, but has retained the charm of a tiny fishing hamlet, and you will still see an old mariner with huge nets stretched the length of the piazza, repairing the gaps with an enormous needle.

3 Sambuca di Sicilia
MAP C3

Featuring lovely Baroque buildings, Arabesque alleyways and a valley of vineyards, Sambuca di Sicilia is easily one of the most picturesque towns in all of Sicily – and without many tourists. In particular, the ruins of Mazzalakar castle, set along Lake Arancia (Orange Lake) are worth a visit.

4 Palazzolo Acreide

Originally a Greek village called Akrai (a small Greek theatre remains), Palazzolo Acreide is an enchanting village in the Hyblean mountains with an impressive range of historic sites to visit, considering its size (see p125). Most of what you see today is Baroque: the churches are spectacular, particularly the large Church of San Sebastiano and the tiny Church of the Annunciation with its ornate twisting columns.

⑤ Butera
MAP E5

High on a plateau overlooking fields out to the sea, Butera dates from the Bronze Age and has traces of Lombard in its dialect. Famous for its acres of vineyards, it supplies grapes to local and national winemakers.

⑥ Piana degli Albanesi
MAP C2

Nestled in the Sicanian hills, this town was founded in the 15th century by Greco-Albanian refugees and has retained its unique heritage. The locals speak in Albanian dialect and street signs are bilingual. Their weddings take place with traditional costumes and Byzantine Catholic rites.

⑦ Mezzojuso
MAP D3

The name of this village translates as "halfway down" – and it is halfway down the Madonie mountains. It has an Alpine rather than a Mediterranean feel. It was home to Greco-Albanian settlers, and the Basilian monastery was a hub of cultural activity; it now houses a library with antique books.

⑧ Petralia Soprana
MAP E3

The highest village in Madonie, at 1,147m (3,760 ft) above sea level, medieval Petralia Soprana feels untouched by the modern world, with vistas of the rolling mountains below.

Petralia Soprana atop the mountains

Winding stone streets of Erice

⑨ Erice

Erice has managed to keep much of its medieval charm. The buildings are all built of locally quarried white stone, adding to its lovely storybook appearance. The stones of the steep streets have characteristic patterns, worn over time *(see p99)*.

⑩ Palazzo Adriano
MAP D3

In the heart of this fertile area, Palazzo Adriano is lofty and remote. In Piazza Umberto I are two churches, Catholic Santa Maria del Lume and the Greek Orthodox Santa Maria Assunta, built in the 1400s. The Italian film *Cinema Paradiso* was set here *(see p57)*.

𝗧𝗢𝗣𝟭𝟬 Beaches

Isolated cove with rocky towers in the sea, near Scopello

① Castellammare del Golfo
MAP C2

The beaches west of Castellammare are prettier and less populated than those to the east. There are beautiful coves with clear water – those with pebble beaches are spectacular in Lo Zingaro *(see p100)* and at Scopello Tonnara, with its rock towers and old boat ramp for sunbathing.

② Mondello
MAP D2

This is Palermo's backyard. It is crowded with the seaside villas of Palermo's aristocracy and locals of all walks of life taking advantage of the beach, bars, *gelaterie*, restaurants and clubs. For swimming, nature and tranquillity, this is not the best beach in Sicily, but it's popular for those who want to be part of the scene.

③ Eraclea Minoa
MAP C4

Below the ruins of the Greek city *(see p118)* a little seaside village comes to life in summer. The sandy beach is long, wide and open, and buffered by pine woods. At either end are two bars providing beach chairs and snacks.

④ Aci Castello
MAP G4

Here clear, blue water laps onto the black lava rocks just below the castle *(see p48)*. Descend to the left, where a water polo court is set up in summer, or to the right to a wooden deck for sunbathing and diving.

⑤ Mazzarò & Giardini Naxos
MAP H3

The water at the two resorts below Taormina is a calm, brilliant blue. The cable car from Taormina descends to Mazzarò, a developed resort area with two pebble beaches lined with well-equipped bathing spots, coves for exploring and the popular island of Isola Bella *(see p18)*. Giardini Naxos is a town with a port and long stretches of beach lined with hotels *(see p109)*.

Beach activities at Mondello

6 Lampedusa
MAP B6

The tiny islet Isola dei Conigli, off Lampedusa, and the bay in between have been set apart as a nature reserve for sea turtles who lay their eggs on the beach. The water is clean and shallow in the bay and the sands are white, but there are no facilities, so bring your own supplies.

7 Scoglitti & Donnalucata
MAP F6

The sandy beaches along this southeast stretch of coast are long and wide and splashed with green-blue surf. There is very little tourist development, beyond small fishing villages including Scoglitti and Donnalucata, with their nice markets and good restaurants, and little seaside villages that come to life in summer, such as Marina di Ragusa.

8 Selinunte
MAP B4

A large sandy beach stretches to the east of the port and just below the temples *(see pp36–9)*. Bathing establishments offer beach chairs, watersports equipment, restaurants and bars. It tends to be crowded with students showing off their skimpy suits and tans, but through the small pine wood to the west you'll find an open beach for families.

9 Pollara, Salina
MAP G1

A crescent of large pebbles with a cliff backdrop. When the wind is high, the beach disappears under the waves, even in summer. There is a *faraglione* (rock tower) poking out of the sea. Bring food and drink or get supplies in the piazza *(see p16)*.

Cliffs of Pollara Beach, Salina

10 Vendicari
MAP G6

A spectacular nature reserve with sandy beaches set around a 15th-century Aragonese tower. The pristine coast here offers a peaceful, natural experience. The park is covered with Mediterranean maquis, and its wetland habitat is a stop for birds migrating to and from Africa.

Following pages The rooftops in the Baroque town of Ragusa

🔟 Outdoor Activities

Hiking on an old lava flow

1 Hiking

There are great hikes all over the island, whether you're looking for a strenuous climb up a volcano, a long walk through the green hills of the interior or an exciting hike on trails clinging to the cliffs above the blue sea. Most nature reserves are *orientata* (orientated), meaning that they have marked trails that may be graded for difficulty. Lo Zingaro has a good selection of trails, as do the parks of the Nebrodi and Madonie mountain ranges *(see pp100 and 113)*. Hire a guide to explore Mount Etna, Stromboli or Vulcano.

Diving off the Egadi Islands

2 Golf

Il Picciolo Golf Club: www. ilpicciologolf.com ▪ Le Madonie Golf Club: www.lemadoniegolf.com ▪ www.italygolfandmore.com ▪ Verdura Golf & Spa Resort: www. verduraresort.com

There are several 18-hole courses in Sicily, often set in dramatic coastal locations. Some courses are part of a luxury hotel complex offering spas, culinary initiatives and cultural events.

3 Fishing, Favignana

You can't join in the traditional *mattanza* fishing ritual, although you can watch it in progress if you happen to be there when the tuna are running *(see p53)*. You can also hire a boat with a local captain for a day's fishing.

4 Watersports

Diving and snorkelling are available with trained guides through diving centres in many places, such as Scopello and the Aeolian Islands, or snorkel on your own to enjoy the marine life along Sicily's shores. Beaches in touristy areas hire out pedal boats and windsurfing boards.

5 Swimming

The unspoiled, clear water off Sicily and the offshore islands is spectacular, and great for swimming. The shoreline has sandy or pebble beaches, private coves, grottoes and rock formations. Lifeguards are not always on duty.

6 Horse Riding

Nature reserves such as Lo Zingaro, the Madonie and Nebrodi mountain ranges and Mount Etna are populated with small farms with horses for hire. Ask at the nearest hotel or check park leaflets for *ippoturismo* and *maneggio* (stables).

Cycling is a good way to explore

7 Cycling

Sicily has a steep terrain for cyclists, though it is a great way to sightsee in the quieter towns and many tourist offices offer free bike hire. Hiring a bicycle on the islands is a convenient way to get around.

8 Exploring Gorges

Natural gorges and canyons are great places for a hike and swim during the hot summer. Companies run tours to the gorges, often as part of a day-long hike. The gorges at Alcàntara, Cava Grande and Gole di Tiberio are especially good.

9 Boating

Sail your own, arriving at one of Sicily's many ports, or hire a boat and a captain for an insider's tour of hidden coves.

10 Skiing on Mount Etna

The depth of snow depends on underground lava flows, but there's enough of a base for winter skiing on the northern slopes. At Zafferana Etnea, Linguaglossa or Nicolosi ski hire, a ski school and lifts are available (see pp20–21).

TOP 10 SICILIAN FLORA AND FAUNA

1 Sea Turtles
Rare sea turtles bury their eggs in the sands of the Belice Estuary and the Pelagie Islands.

2 Sanfratellano Horse
A species indigenous to the Nebrodi, descendant of ancient *Equus sicanus*.

3 Cirneco dell'Etna
The native dog of Mount Etna is a natural hunter who seeks small prey.

4 Cactus
The *fico d'India*, or prickly pear, thrives in Sicily's arid climate.

5 Dwarf Palm
This tiny palm flourishes in the northwest of Sicily; its fronds are preferred by craftsmen for weaving baskets and brooms.

6 Fennel
Bright yellow, fluffy green or tall and crispy brown, depending upon the season, it covers hillsides and springs up along the side of roads.

7 Agave
The low-growing aloe-like plant with curling spiky leaves puts out a central stalk that can reach up to 12 m (40 ft).

8 Thistle
The hearty, spiky plant pops up along roadsides and in fields with its bright purple flowers – not to be confused with cultivated artichokes.

9 Forests
The few remains of once-prevalent pine, oak, cork-oak and beech forests are now carefully protected.

10 Girgentana Goat
This breed from the Agrigento area has long, twisting horns and is bred specially for its milk.

Girgentana goats and kids

Children's Attractions

1 Puppet Theatres

Puppet theatres offer gory re-enactments of crusader sword fights, and encourage the audience to root for a favourite crusader. The puppets "speak" in Italian, or Sicilian dialect, but it's easy enough to follow the action *(see pp68–9)*.

Museo di Geologia "G G Gemmellaro"

2 Museo di Geologia "G G Gemmellaro", Palermo

MAP L6 ▪ Corso Tukori 131 ▪ 091 23864665 ▪ Open summer: 9am–1pm Mon–Sat; winter: 9am–1pm & 3–5pm Mon–Fri, 9am–1pm Sat ▪ Closed Aug

Palermo's impressive geological museum fascinates children and adults alike with displays from its collection of over 600,000 artifacts and specimens. These include remains of the elephants that roamed Sicily in the Pleistocene era; a quartz crystal containing a drop of Mediterranean seawater over 5 million years old; the skeleton of a woman, known as Thea, dating from the late Stone Age.

3 Castles

Sicily's castles are rich in history and intrigue, with trapdoors, secret passageways, dungeons, spy windows and hidden places from which boiling oil was once poured onto the enemy *(see pp48–9)*.

4 Museo del Sale, Paceco

South of Trapani, the small salt museum is inside a windmill. Its fascinating exhibits show how the windmill transfers water from pool to pool and grinds the harvested salt. Work in the saltpans is ongoing, and you can see each stage that turns sea water to table salt. There is a restaurant on site *(see p102)*.

5 Museo del Cinema, Catania

MAP G4 ▪ Piazzale Rocco Chinnici, "Le Ciminiere" ▪ 095 4011928 ▪ Open 9am–5pm Tue–Sun; Jul & Aug: 10am–6pm (last entry 5pm) ▪ Adm

Catania's child- and adult-friendly museum celebrates the cinematic arts and its history. Educational and fun, exhibits retell the story of an enduring love affair between cinema and Sicily *(see p57)*.

6 Etnaland, Belpasso

MAP G4 ▪ 095 7913334 ▪ Open late Jun–early Sep: 9:30am–6:30pm daily ▪ Adm ▪ www.etnaland.eu

Sicily's top theme park has a full-size dinosaur park and plenty of water rides, including the Crocodile Rapids. There are rides for the youngest children, and others that will get the adrenaline flowing in even the most hardened theme park veteran.

Gentle rides for young children at Etnaland

7 Motya

The archaeological park on the island of Motya requires a short boat ride across the lagoon (less than 10 minutes each way). The spacious park shows inquisitive kids how the Phoenicians and the Carthaginians lived *(see p101)*.

8 Museo dell'Etna, Viagrande

MAP G3 ▪ Via Dietro Serra 6 ▪ 095 7890768 ▪ Open 9am–12:30pm Mon–Fri by reservation, Sat & Sun groups only

This interactive museum uses 3D models and satellite images to explain volcanic phenomena in a fun and interesting way *(see pp20–21)*.

Studying volcanoes, Museo dell'Etna

9 Nature Reserves

Sicily's nature reserves are good places to spot wildlife, picnic, swim or use the graded hiking trails. Mount Etna *(see pp20–21)* is probably the most fascinating – the volcano is always smoking, if not throwing red sparks into the air. Guides give a lively account of lava flow and the gift shops screen spectacular video footage.

10 Aquarium, Syracuse

MAP H5 ▪ Largo Aretusa, Ortygia ▪ Open 10am–8pm daily ▪ Adm

The Syracuse *Acquario* has 40 tanks of marine life from the Mediterranean, freshwater and tropical habitats. It is at the Fonte Aretusa, on the island of Ortygia; entry is from the marina.

TOP 10 FAMILY-FRIENDLY THEME PARKS

Parco Adventura Etna

1 Parco Avventura Etna, Milo
Climb into treehouses and slide down chutes at this adventure park, or simply go for a walk, near Mount Etna.

2 Città del Mare, Terrasini
Boasting the highest water slide in Europe, this park guarantees fun and relaxation for the whole family.

3 L'EcoCampus Casaboli
This adventure park near Palermo allows children to climb trees and rope ladders, and enjoy a picnic in the forest.

4 Parco Avventura Madonie, Petralia Sottana
This adventure park is the place to spend the day learning about nature while sharpening your acrobatic skills.

5 Agriturismo Bergi, Castelbuono
Spend the day enjoying a delicious meal at this farmhouse while kids learn about the day-to-day life on a farm.

6 Giardino Inglese, Palermo
In the heart of the city, this urban park features rides and a roller-skating rink.

7 Acquapark Sommatino
On long hot summer days, this waterpark is an ideal place to escape from the heat.

8 Bioparco di Sicilia, Carini
See dinosaur replicas, exotic animals and rare flora while learning about the dangers of extinction.

9 Nebrodi Adventure Park, Longi
Slide down ropes and learn about bird watching, then go for a walk in the fresh Nebrodi air.

10 Parcallario, Buccheri
Have an adventurous day in the Hyblean hills while learning about local flora and fauna.

🔟 Puppet Traditions

Puppet theatre in Monreale

1 Origins

There were puppeteers in ancient Syracuse, but the Opera dei Pupi as we know it today became popular in the 1800s. Puppet theatres provided entertainment for thousands of Sicilians – Palermo had more than 25 theatres where crowds would watch stories of adventure and romance. Travelling puppet theatres drew huge crowds in villages.

2 UNESCO Intangible Cultural Heritage

To protect Sicily's unique folk art tradition, Opera dei Pupi was added to UNESCO's Intangible Cultural Heritage of Humanity list in 2008. Sicilian puppet theatres are often family-run affairs, crafting the *burattini* (puppets or marionettes) using methods passed down for generations.

3 Festival di Morgana, Palermo

This international puppet festival, held in November, promotes traditional as well as contemporary puppetry, and brings together artists and theatre companies from around the globe.

4 Catanese School

Puppets of the Catania tradition are almost 1.5 m (5 ft) tall. Puppeteers manoeuvre the heavy puppets via a metal pole attached to the heads, moving their limbs with strings. The puppets' joints are fixed and the swords of the paladins are drawn. They inhabit a narrow stage with a long horizontal backdrop and are sometimes joined by live actors.

5 Palermitan School

Palermitan puppets are around 1 m (3 ft) tall. They are entirely handled by strings, have movable joints, can raise their face guards and draw their swords at will. They are easily manipulated and their sword fights are more lively. The stage of the Palermo-style theatre is a deeply recessed space with room for many characters and decorated scenery.

6 Stories

Productions relate saints' lives, Shakespearean themes, stories of bandits and local farces. The most traditional subjects are derived from the epic poems of the Carolingian cycle, retold by Ludovico Ariosto in his 1516 *Orlando Furioso*. The Holy Roman Emperor Charlemagne and his paladins battle for Christianity against the Saracens and Turks.

Scene at the Festival di Morgana

7 "The Bad Guys"
Saracens and Turks wear baggy trousers and moustaches and bear shields with a crescent moon. Charlemagne's brother-in-law and arch-enemy Gano di Magonza tries to overthrow the crown. Sorcerer Malagigi plays both sides, helping and hurting the paladins' cause.

8 "The Good Guys"
The Holy Roman Emperor Charlemagne and his paladins wear armour and skirts. Orlando carries a shield with a cross. His cousin Rinaldo, a brave fighter, has a lion on his shield, as does his warrior sister Bradamante. Angelica, the object of the two men's affections, is usually at their side.

Puppets in their armour

9 Assedio a Parigi
In this very traditional story, Charlemagne, under siege by the Turks, sends Rinaldo to prepare the French army and another warrior to Rome to ask assistance from the Pope. Rinaldo defeats the Turkish leader. Malagigi prompts Orlando and Rinaldo to end their differences and face the Saracens in Paris. Orlando saves the day.

10 The Defeat of Roncisvalle and the Death of Orlando
In a famous tale, Charlemagne is tricked by his brother-in-law Gano and the paladins find themselves outnumbered. After putting up a noble fight, Orlando dies.

TOP 10 PUPPET PLACES AND PEOPLE

Handmade puppets

1 Museo Internazionale delle Marionette Antonio Pasqualino, Palermo
This museum houses fine puppets, stages and sets *(see p94)*.

2 Museo Civico dell'Opera dei Pupi, Sortino
The collection of the Puglisi family, *pupari* (puppeteers) for five generations.

3 Opera dei Pupi di Enzo Mancuso, Palermo
Opened in 1928 by Enzo Mancuso, it is now operated by his grandson *(see p71)*.

4 Opera dei Pupi, Syracuse
The Vaccaro-Mauceri company has performed puppet shows for generations *(see p71)*.

5 Teatro dell'Opera dei Pupi Mimmo Cuticchio, Palermo
Giacomo Cuticchio's legacy lives on through the work of Mimmo Cuticchio.

6 Marionettistica Fratelli Napoli, Catania
Gaetano Napoli founded the Catanese puppet theatre in 1921.

7 Mimmo Cuticchio and Virgilio Sieni
A performance uniting contemporary dance and puppetry.

8 Teatro dei Pupi Siciliani-Famiglia Argento, Palmero
The Argento family has been performing across from Palermo's Cathedral since 1893.

9 Salamanca, Catania
Francesco Salamanca is a restorer and collector of Sicilian puppets.

10 Anna Cuticchio: First Female Puppeteer, Palermo
The daughter of Mimmo Cuticchio once owned a theatre and manipulated over 60 puppets.

Performing Arts Venues

1 Teatro Antico di Taormina

Resting on the acropolis of ancient Taormenium and famed for its views, this Greco-Roman theatre is a magnificent outdoor performance venue (see p18). Its programme begins with the Taormina Film Festival in early summer and the theatre also hosts concerts by international artists.

Ancient amphitheatre, Taormina

2 Lo Spasimo, Palermo

The open nave of Santa Maria dello Spasimo alla Kalsa, a former church, is a romantic venue for performances and film. Music can be heard from the upper outdoor terrace as well, while artworks are on display in the covered exhibition space (see p96).

3 Archaeological Park, Selinunte

During August performances of Greek drama, classical and modern dance, and music are staged among the ruins in Selinunte's archaeological park. Performances start at 9pm (see pp36–7).

4 Teatro Massimo Bellini, Catania

MAP G4 ■ **Via Perrotta 12**

Catania's great opera house, named after local composer Vincenzo Bellini (see p56), opened its doors in 1890. The season of opera and concerts, including chamber music, and ballet performances by the theatre ballet company, runs from October to June.

5 Teatro Massimo, Palermo

The Teatro Massimo was built in the 1880s as a symbol of post-Unification Sicily by Neo-Classical architects Giovanni Battista Basile and his son Ernesto. Despite its grandeur and superb acoustics, the theatre fell into decline. After a massive renovation effort, the doors were reopened in 1997, and once again it is Palermo's premier venue for classical music, ballet and opera (see p96).

6 Opera dei Pupi, Syracuse

MAP H5 ■ **Via della Giudecca 22**
■ **www.teatrodeipupisiracusa.it**

Puppeteers Mauceri and Vaccaro direct traditional puppet shows in the Catania style *(see p68)*; as well as the lives of the saints, there are the Mauceri family's own productions. You can also watch puppets being made and restored in the family workshop.

7 Teatro Ditirammu, Palermo

MAP P4 ■ **Via Torremuzza 6** ■ **www.teatroditirammu.it**

This 52-seat theatre in Palermo's historic Kalsa district stages concerts of Sicilian folk music. It also promotes shows of lively tarantella or heart-wrenching storytelling set to music throughout the city – outdoors in Piazza Kalsa, for example.

8 Opera dei Pupi di Enzo Mancuso, Palermo

MAP L1 ■ **Via Collegio di Maria al Borgo Vecchio 17** ■ **091 8146971** ■ **www.mancusopupi.it**

The Mancuso family has been working with Sicilian puppets since 1928, and young Enzo dedicates himself to breathing new life into the art. He makes puppets as needed, but his collection also includes vintage models that have been passed down.

Traditional puppet tale

Stage at the Greek Theatre, Syracuse

9 Greek Theatre, Syracuse

Classical works are staged in spring in Syracuse's ancient theatre, including Aeschylus's tragedies, premiered here thousands of years ago. Daily performances take place from mid-May through to the end of June. The largest theatre of ancient Sicily is mostly intact and fits modern stage sets and seating *(see p25)*.

10 Teatro Luigi Pirandello, Agrigento

MAP D4 ■ **Piazza Luigi Pirandello 1** ■ **www.teatroluigipirandello.it**

The ornate Agrigento civic theatre was opened in 1880. The venue was dedicated to the playwright Luigi Pirandello on the 10th anniversary of his death in 1946 *(see p57)*. From November to May there are modern theatre performances and dance, as well as works by Pirandello.

Nights Out

Jazz club in Palermo

Clubs
Discoteche open up each summer, often under new names and management from previous years. Huge crowds of visitors mix with locals to fill up the open-air dance floors and bars. Look for posters for clubs, especially in towns and villages close to the sea.

2 The Piazza
In villages in summer when people stay inside during hot after-noons, families and friends sit in the piazza and eat *gelato* into the night. In touristy towns, the piazza has a pub atmosphere with live music and outdoor tables, such as the Caffè del Molo and Bar al Duomo at Cefalù.

3 The Passeggiata
The *passeggiata* (promenade) can be an afternoon or an evening activity. In summer, join the crowds on the promenades at Selinunte, San Vito lo Capo, Mondello, Marina di Ragusa, Palermo (Via Ruggero Settimo) and Catania (Via Etnea).

4 Associazione Culturale Palab, Palermo
This lively cultural centre stages live music, comedy, theatre, dance, film and exhibitions of contemporary art and photography. There's a cocktail bar, pizzeria and restaurant *(see p96)*.

5 Via Landolina, Catania
MAP G4

Via Landolina, near the Piazza Bellini, is lined with bars and clubs. La Chiave (Nos. 64–70) usually has a programme of live music and in summer organizes Landolina Live, a full slate of live rock, folk and jazz during June, July and August.

6 I Candelai, Palermo
MAP K4 ■ Via dei Candelai 65

This Palermo dive has been going strong since 1996. Popular as a venue for live acts, arts events and tango lessons, it's a favourite with students from the nearby university.

Pavement cafés near Piazza Olivella, Palermo

7 Agorà, Catania
MAP G4 ▪ Piazza Currò 6

This lively bar and restaurant owes its unique atmosphere to the cool stream of water flowing through its cave area. The site has been in use since ancient Roman times, and now it lies below Catania's youth hostel (see p147), in the centre of town, beside the fish market.

Airy Kursaal Kalhesa restaurant

8 Kursaal Kalhesa, Palermo
MAP P5 ▪ Foro Umberto I 21 ▪ 340 157 3493 ▪ www.kursaalkalhesa.it

A bar, restaurant, café, music venue and bookshop in one, this place is housed in a 15th-century *palazzo*. It has an outdoor restaurant attracting an eclectic crowd. It is LGBT friendly.

9 Zo, Catania
MAP G4 ▪ Piazzale Asia 6 ▪ 095 7463122 ▪ www.zoculture.it

This dynamic arts and cultural centre is located in the same former sulphur works as Le Ciminiere (see p51). It hosts local and international performances of music, dance and theatre, as well as temporary exhibitions. There is a café and restaurant, too.

10 Lapis
▪ www.lapis.it

This free publication has complete listings of music, theatre and art events. Separate editions are printed in Palermo and Catania.

TOP 10 FEATURES OF THE PASSEGGIATA

1 The Walk
The key to the walk on the *passeggiata* is to do it *very* slowly.

2 See
Everybody checks out everybody else for everything from physical attributes to their fashion sense to how well behaved their children are.

3 Be Seen
Wear the latest fashions, whether Dolce & Gabbana catwalk originals or market-stall copies.

4 When and Where
The prime time is Sunday afternoon or any day from dusk onwards. Walk around a piazza, down a *corso* or promenade, or anywhere people happen to gather.

5 Who
From babies in prams to teens to grandparents, to entire families, couples and groups of friends, this is an open event.

6 The Touch
Everyone holds hands or entwines arms with their walking partners.

7 Food
The only things the Italians consume while in motion are *gelato* or peanuts or similar small snacks.

8 Men with Earpieces
Pocket radios allow sports fans to stay abreast of the *partita* (football match) or Formula Uno motor racing.

9 By Car
Locals drive the *passeggiata* with the windows down so that they can chat.

10 Spectator Sport
If you prefer, feel free to sit and watch the *passeggiata* go by. A table outside a café is the perfect spot.

Piazza IX Aprile in Taormina

Wines and Wine Producers

1 Monreale
MAP C2

Monreale has produced fine wines for centuries from indigenous grapes, such as Perricone, Inzolia, and Catarratto, as well as Chardonnay. Try at the Calatrasi Principe di Camporeale or Sellier de la Tour.

Marsala wine in production

2 Marsala

A fortified wine produced in Marsala since the 18th century *(see p101)*. A DOC *(Denominazione di Origine Controllata)* was awarded in 1986. Marsala is produced as Fine, Superiore (aged at least two years), Riserva (aged at least four years) or Vergine and Soleras (aged at least 10 years). From Inzolia, Catarratto and Grillo grapes, the wine is amber with a citrus flower and almond perfume.

3 Nero d'Avola

This is the classic Sicilian red, made from at least 80 per cent of grapes of the same name with added Perricone, and characterized by its intense ruby colour and flavour of aromatic herbs. It's produced over the entire eastern half of the island but the two largest producers are between Palermo and Cefalù: Regaleali and Duca di Salaparuta.

4 Artisan Producers

Many artisan producers are making great wines. Look out for COS, Fondo Antico, Occhipinti, Graci, Frank Cornelissen, Palari, Girolamo Russo, La Moresca and Terra delle Sirene.

5 Malvasia and Passito

Producers on Salina leave their Malvasia delle Lipari grapes to dry out on the vine or on mats to concentrate the flavours to make a dessert wine that is thick and sweet. Pantelleria's Zibibbo grapes are treated in a similar way, left on the vine until the flavours have condensed to make a dessert wine with intense tastes of dried fruits and vanilla.

6 Bianco d'Alcamo

Eighty per cent Catarratto with a dash of Damaschino, Grecanico and Trebbiano make up this dry and fruity white. Abundant production (more grapes are grown in Trapani than any other Sicilian province) made this the classic Sicilian white. The area from San Vito Lo Capo to Castellammare and inland to Alcamo and Calatafimi is under DOC protection.

Road through Alcamo vineyards

7 Regaleali
MAP E3

This estate has been in the Tasca d'Almerita family since 1830. Famous for traditional Sicilian wines, their reds, based on Nero d'Avola, include Regaleali Rosso and the Rosso del Conte; whites, mainly of Inzolia and their own Varietà Tasca, include Villa Tasca and Nozze d'Oro.

Regaleali's Nero d'Avola

8 Erice

This wine is from grapes in the Erice valley, and varieties run from white to red to sweet dessert (passito). One of the best is the Syrah from the Casa Vinicola Fazio winery.

Vineyards near the base of Etna

9 Etna Bianco and Etna Rosso

Sicily's first DOC was awarded in 1968 to the southern and eastern zone of Mount Etna, where the white grapes Cataratto and Carricante flourish. Reds, mostly the Nerello Mascalese, grow at the volcano's base.

10 Cerasuolo di Vittoria

The cherry-red, dry and fruity wine is made from an interesting blend of Frappato, Calabrese and Nerello grapes grown near Vittoria in Ragusa. Established producers are buying vineyards here to produce their own versions of Cerasuolo.

TOP 10 GRAPE VARIETIES

Bunch of Zibibbo grapes

1 Zibibbo
The grape of Pantelleria, used traditionally for the sweet passito, is now also popular for crisp white wines.

2 Nero d'Avola
This powerhouse Sicilian red grape is cultivated in the eastern half of the island.

3 Frappato
Cultivated in Ragusa province, the primary grape of Cerasuolo di Vittoria.

4 Grillo
A white grape indigenous to western Sicily and the basis of Marsala and other whites.

5 Inzolia
Also called Ansonica, a white grape found throughout western Sicily, used in Marsala and other wines.

6 Nerello Mascalese
Primary red grape grown on the slopes of Mount Etna, blended with Nerello Cappuccio to make the deep, spicy Etna Rosso.

7 Malvasia di Lipari
Responsible for the fragrant wines of Salina, rich in flavours of almond and candied fruits.

8 Catarratto
A white grape grown from Marsala to Alcamo, Salina and Etna. Its character changes depending on the microclimate.

9 Grecanico
White grape native to western Sicily and one of the primary components of Bianco d'Alcamo.

10 Pollico
The oldest variety known on the island, these white grapes are used to make Moscato wine.

🔟 Sicilian Dishes

Sardines stuffed with breadcrumbs and raisins

3 Pasta

The amazing variety of pasta dishes available makes use of all the bounty that Sicily has to offer. A typical Palermitan dish is *pasta con le sarde* (with sardines, fennel, pine nuts, raisins and anchovies). The pasta itself, made with local durum wheat, is firm and full of flavour.

1 Fish and Seafood

There is always an excellent choice of fish and seafood in Sicily. Look out for *sogliola* (sole), *triglie* (red mullet), *pesce spada* (swordfish), *tonno* (tuna), *mazzancolla* (large sweet prawns), *aragosta* (spiny lobster), *sarde* (sardines), *polpo* (octopus), *calamaro* (squid) and *gambero rosso* (red prawns).

4 Spleen Sandwiches

It takes a lot of curiosity to choose to sink your teeth into this classic street food staple. The sandwich can be either plain (*schettu*, single) or topped with grated cheese (*maritatu*, married). More daring versions come with crunchy trachea bits.

2 Caponata

Originally a fish dish, *caponata* was adapted by the *cucina povera* (kitchen of the poor) as a slow-cooked mix of aubergine (eggplant), tomato, celery, capers, olives, raisins and pine nuts, flavoured with vinegar and sugar, and topped with toasted almonds.

Lemon ice cream

5 Gelato

The reason Sicilian ice cream (*gelato*) is so special is its base: a *crema* developed from Arab and Spanish culinary influences that is made with milk, or almond milk, as well as starch. It produces a rich, smooth and light dessert (*see p110*).

6 Cassata and Cannoli

These classic Sicilian desserts are made with lightly sweetened ricotta. In *cassata*, ricotta and sponge cake are covered with marzipan and decorated with candied fruits. *Cannoli* are fried pastry shells filled with ricotta, candied fruit and chocolate chips.

7 Meat

Excellent lamb and pork are produced in Sicily. Sausages are always spiced and made with *semi di finocchio* (fennel seeds), stuffed in narrow casings and formed into continuous coils.

Traditional Sicilian *caponata*

8 Panelle

Another snack food available from street vendors are these small squares of fried batter made from chickpea flour and a sprinkling of parsley, then topped with salt and lemon juice. They are often served in a sandwich.

9 Arancini

A Sicilian fast-food treat that is available in bars and from street vendors. Balls of rice are stuffed with a meaty tomato or vegetable *ragù* or with ham and cheese, rolled in breadcrumbs, and fried.

Tasty, round, golden *arancini*

10 Bread

Bread in Sicily is made from *grano duro* (semolina flour), and once baked it is dense and golden. The shapes are particular too, including braided loaves. Bread is used in main dishes – *mollica* are spiced and toasted breadcrumbs, used instead of cheese on top of pasta. Look for *sfincione*, similar to a thick-crust pizza eaten as a snack, and *focacce*, thin baked layers of dough filled with greens, sausage, ricotta or tomato.

Bread in an array of shapes

TOP 10 LOCAL PRODUCE

Sicilian blood oranges

1 Citrus Fruits
Excellent lemons (there is a small, sweet variety) and oranges (with numerous blood-red varieties) abound.

2 Cheese
Sicilian cheese comes from cow's or sheep's milk. Look for *primo sale* or aged *pecorino, tuma, caciocavallo* and *Ragusano*.

3 Ricotta
A cheese by-product used for sweet and savoury dishes. Available fresh, baked, or salted and aged (called *ricotta salata*).

4 Capers
From tiny buds to the huge *cucunci,* the best come from Salina and Pantelleria.

5 Vegetables
Amazing bounty awaits at market-places and restaurants. Don't miss the long skinny *cucuzza* (squash) and spicy red garlic.

6 Salt
Richly flavoured salt has been harvested from the sea near Trapani since Phoenician times.

7 Durum Wheat
The secret behind Sicily's flavourful bread and pasta. The countryside is covered with wheat fields.

8 Almonds and Pistachios
Eastern Sicily is known for its production of these high-quality and richly flavoured nuts.

9 Tuna
You'll find this fish preserved in oil and fresh in a variety of cuts.

10 Olives and Olive Oil
Millions of olive trees produce excellent-quality table olives and thick, green aromatic olive oil.

Restaurants

1 Majore, Chiaramonte Gulfi

It's worth the trek to Majore, perched on a hilltop with fine views over the Ragusa plains. This simple restaurant, in the back of a butcher's shop, has been serving the finest pork dishes since 1896, including a range of salami antipasti *(see p131)*.

Majore is through the doorway

2 Ristorante Duomo, Ragusa Ibla

Chef Ciccio Sultano carefully selects ingredients for his traditional Ragusan dishes, but adds his own twist. In three small, bright dining rooms, every course is excellent. Two different tasting menus let you try a bit of everything *(see p131)*.

3 Piccolo Napoli, Palermo

Arguably the best fish restaurant in town, Piccolo Napoli serves up only the freshest catches of the day and pairs them with locally sourced ingredients. Start with a hearty portion of *linguine alle vongole*, followed by a main of *sarde a beccafico*, all washed down with a local white wine *(see p97)*.

4 Ristorante Fidone Maria, Frigintini

Maria Fidone and her family can be found in the kitchen at their homely trattoria, preparing hearty Ragusan meals for dinner. Everything is made in-house, including the pasta, bread, olive oil and liqueurs. For a first course, choose the thick broad-bean soup *(lolli)* or homemade pasta. For a second course, try stuffed chicken accompanied by stuffed aubergines (eggplants) *(see p131)*.

5 La Cialoma, Marzamemi

In the great atmosphere of the piazza of Marzamemi, La Cialoma occupies the ancient tuna fishery of Prince Villadorata's family. The name is a Sicilian term for the work songs sung by tuna fishermen of old. La Cialoma has a small menu and a big wine list. The food is fresh, simple and nicely prepared: try the excellent marinated sardines or, in season, the simple and delectable tuna braised with laurel *(see p131)*.

Tables in the piazza at La Cialoma, Marzamemi

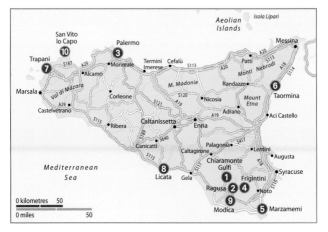

6 Osteria Nero d'Avola, Taormina

Creative yet unimposing dishes of local fish come from the open kitchen. Turi the chef is a hunter, so look for game in season. He offers seasonal and local ingredients prepared well and without too many flourishes. The restaurant also stands out for its reasonable prices, which is rare in Taormina (see p115).

The calm interior of Accursio

7 Cantina Siciliana, Trapani

Chef Pino Maggiore serves Trapani's classic *kus kus al pesce* (fish couscous) in a quaint interior in the old Jewish ghetto. He also offers pasta dishes (including the sublime *pesto alla Trapanese*, with tomatoes, garlic, almonds and basil), mains and desserts (try ricotta-filled *cassateddi*). The wine list is Sicilian (see p105).

9 Accursio, Modica

This Michelin-starred restaurant is set within an old *palazzo* in the heart of Modica. The head chef uses the best of Sicily's land-based and seafood produce, then puts a modern twist on the classics. The *arancino*, for example, is served on a plate and stuffed with ricotta and prawns (see p131).

8 La Madia, Licata

Chef Pino Cuttaia's dishes dazzle. The seven-course tasting menu is a culinary experience that merits his two Michelin stars. A cuttlefish "egg" served with squid ink couscous is a typically inventive dish (see p123).

Seafood dish at La Madia

10 Pocho, San Vito lo Capo

The terrace at Pocho offers pretty views of Monte Cofano and the bay. The restaurant's owner, Marilú Terrasi, is well-known for her couscous, and the extensive wine list is made up of selected Sicilian labels (see p105).

For a key to restaurant price ranges see p97

Pasticcerie and Gelaterie

① Verona & Bonvegna, Catania

MAP G4 ■ Via Asiago 60

Undoubtedly the best *pasticceria* and *gelateria* in Catania, and one of the very best in Sicily. You can watch the skilled pastry chefs at work, creating mouthwatering masterpieces such as little filled ricotta doughnuts and their famed *cannoli*. Takeaway only, and there may well be a queue.

Fruit pastries at Pasticceria Cappello

② Cistercian Monastery, Agrigento

The nuns at the monastery of the Santo Spirito still offer pastries from behind the grate. They may look like something you've seen at other shops, but take a bite and taste how special they are. Order ahead for the speciality, sweet couscous *(see p33)*.

③ Pasticceria Russo, Santa Venerina, near Catania

MAP G4 ■ Via Vittorio Emanuele 105

Since 1880 the Russo family has been making Catanese pastries with fine local ingredients, such as honey, pistachios, almonds and oranges.

Elegant interior of Pasticceria Russo

④ Pasticceria Cappello, Palermo

MAP K1 ■ Via Colonna Rotta 68;
MAP J2 ■ Via Nicolo Garzilli 19

Two branches sell among the best pastries in Palermo. The *setteveli* cake, featuring seven different-flavoured chocolate layers, is an unmissable experience.

⑤ Pasticceria Artigianale Grammatico Maria, Erice

Maria Grammatico spent many years in the orphanage inside Erice's cloistered San Carlo monastery, learning the nuns' centuries-old recipes for their *dolci*, the sale of which provided their keep. The sweets are the opposite of monastic life: colourful and luxurious. Try *sospiri* (sighs), *cuori* (hearts) and *cuscinetti* (little pillows; see p104).

⑥ Caffè Sicilia, Noto

MAP G5 ■ Corso Vittorio Emanuele 125

For more than a century, the Assenza family has been at work in the maze-like laboratory of the Caffè Sicilia. They hunt down the highest-quality ingredients in the region, working to preserve the Sicilian pastry-making tradition. They create pastries from the recipes of Noto's ex-monastery of Santa Chiara as well as from their own recipes, such as chocolates with carob, chestnut or sweet basil filling, *giuggolena* (sesame seed, honey and orange zest bar) and herb-infused honey.

7 Gelateria Stancampiano, Palermo

MAP D2 ▪ Via Giovanni Campolo 94

This unassuming family-owned shop has the creamiest *gelato* in Sicily. The bow-tied staff proudly offer rows and rows of traditional and seasonal flavours served in cones, cups and brioches. It's worth the walk.

8 Antica Dolceria Bonajuto, Modica

MAP G6 ▪ Corso Umberto I 159

Fig-filled *nucatoli* and citrus and honey *torrone* are displayed in this small, elegant shop. Their chocolate is still made using the ancient Aztec method of working the cocoa with sugar and spices.

Treats at Antica Dolceria Bonajuto

9 Donna Elvira Dolceria, Modica

MAP G6 ▪ Via Risorgimento 32

Elvira Roccasalva reproduces by hand the sweets formerly made by Modica's cloistered nuns. She also uses the best-quality ingredients from the region to create her own recipes: try the *carato*, made with carob flour, raisins and almonds.

10 Pasticceria Arturo, Randazzo

MAP G3 ▪ Via Umberto 73

This pastry shop specializes in sweets made with local pistachios, Sicilian almonds and hazelnuts. Try the spicy pistachio pastries and excellent granita while sitting in the marble interior or outside, enjoying the view.

TOP 10 DESSERTS

Cassata with spring flowers

1 Cassata
Layers of sponge cake and ricotta cream covered with colourful marzipan and candied fruits *(see p76)*.

2 Gelato
Try soft and creamy *gelato*, *zabaglione*, *semifreddo* or the solid *pezzo duro*.

3 Gelo di Melone
The delectable watermelon jelly is infused with jasmine essence and topped with chocolate chips.

4 Cannoli
Ricotta cream of different flavours in fried pastry tubes *(see p76)*.

5 Frutta di Martorana
Marzipan sculpted and painted to look like real fruit or other edibles.

6 Biscotti della Regina
Hard biscuits rolled in sesame seeds.

7 Cassateddi
Fried pastry pockets filled with ricotta flavoured with chocolate, lemon or cinnamon, eaten at breakfast time.

8 Coseduce or Cuccidati
Traditional fig-filled biscuits that exist under various names in every part of the island. Elaborate versions are made for St Joseph's Day *(see p86)* and called *squartucciati*.

9 'Mpanatigghi
These Modican *empanadas*, imported by the Spanish Counts, are a pastry crust filled with chocolate, spices and ground beef.

10 Granita
Ice is added to flavourings such as jasmine, wild strawberry or almond.

Orange granita

🔟 Specialist Shops and Areas

Catania's premier shopping area around Via Etnea

① Palermo and Catania

On and around Palermo's Via della Libertà *(see p95)* and Catania's Via Etnea *(see p114)* you can shop in Italy's fashionable, classic stores for household linens, clothing, shoes and handbags. Both boulevards offer a mix of stores, boutiques and chic cafés.

② Le Colonne, Taormina

Here you'll find elegant jewellery on Taormina's Corso. The proprietor makes each piece crafted to her own design, inspired by antique and historical motifs. Chunky necklaces of heavy gold with precious gems and rings set with antique incised stones are all unique items *(see p114)*.

③ Ceramiche d'Arte F.lli Soldano, Sciacca

MAP C4 ■ Piazza Saverio Friscia 15

Alongside shops selling Sciacca's traditional green, yellow and blue ceramic dishes, the Soldano family produces traditional ceramics and modern designs on tableware and tiles.

④ Ceramiche De Simone, Palermo

This shop sells brightly coloured ceramics with designs of jolly peasant farmers and fishermen going about their daily tasks *(see p95)*.

⑤ Silva Ceramica, Caltagirone

MAP F4 ■ Piazza Umberto I, 19

In a courtyard off the piazza, Silva Ceramica produces imitations of antique designs, including tiles.

⑥ Altieri 1882, Erice

Altieri produces ceramics in traditional styles as well as with their own innovative designs. There are also pieces in gold, silver and coral made in the decorative arts tradition of the Trapani region *(see p104)*.

Unique jewellery from Le Colonne

⑦ Farrugio Design, Catania

MAP G4 ■ Via Ughetti 3

The artisan craft of jewellery making has been handed down from father to son at Farrugio. They are considered one of the finest goldsmiths in Italy.

8 Siculamente, Ragusa
MAP F5 ■ Piazza Duomo 11

Run by three young Sicilian entrepreneurs, here you can buy "T-scierts", caps, buttons and such with intriguing designs full of anti-Mafia symbolism and poignant sayings in Sicilian dialect. These include the fatalistic *Futtatinni* (Don't worry about it) or this romantic description of Sicily: *Unni l'aceddi ci vannu a cantari e li sireni ci fannu l'amuri* (Where the birds go to sing and the mermaids go to make love).

9 Enoteca Picone, Palermo

To call Enoteca Picone a "wine bar" would hardly do it justice. Founded in the 1940s, it started life as a hole-in-the-wall that sold wine directly from the cask to the consumer, but now it is the place to go for its range of over 500 Sicilian, Italian and international wines. It's popular for pre-dinner drinks, where you can sample your choice of wine accompanied by a platter of local meats and cheeses (see p95).

"Non-Mafia" goods at Punto Pizzo Free

10 Punto Pizzo Free, L'Emporio, Palermo

An emporium in the heart of the city selling traditional products, books and crafts gathered from shops around Palermo whose owners have banded together refusing to pay the *pizzo* (the infamous Mafia protection money). There's safety in numbers, but these people are still on the front line, and their courage cannot be overstated. Buy a T-shirt, support the cause (see p95).

TOP 10 MARKETS

Produce at La Vucciria market

1 La Vucciria, Palermo
MAP M4
One of Palermo's oldest markets, where vendors really put on a show.

2 Trapani
MAP B2
Each morning fishermen arrange their catch along the wharf, yelling out its merits or holding it aloft.

3 Selinunte
MAP B4
A lively 7am fish auction. Don't miss it.

4 Ballarò, Palermo
MAP L6
Palermo's most interesting market sells fish, produce and household goods.

5 Del Capo, Palermo
MAP J4
Step back into 19th-century Palermo in the Mandamento del Capo streets, crowded with farmers, housewives, butchers and every sort of meat.

6 Syracuse, Ortygia
MAP H5
Rows of mussels, cherries, almonds, lemons – or whatever is in season.

7 Sciacca
MAP C4
Monday to Friday, in the afternoon, fishermen sell their catch on the wharf.

8 Donnalucata
MAP F6
Each morning, under awnings along the wharf, fishermen sell their catch.

9 Catania
MAP G4
Catania's market is famous for the variety of fish and the rowdy vendors.

10 Impromptu Markets
All over Sicily, farmers sell their own produce, such as artichokes, lemons or cheese from the side of the road.

Sicily for Free

1 Roman Ruins, Palermo
MAP K6 ▪ Within Villa Bonanno, Piazza della Vittoria

Not as extensive and lavish as the villa at Piazza Armerina *(see p30)*, this site nonetheless offers a glimpse into Roman daily life in the late 2nd century AD – with vivid mosaic floors, statues, spas and outdoor latrines.

2 Byzantine church in a Roman bathhouse, Catania
MAP G4 ▪ Piazza Mecca ▪ 095 7150 508 ▪ Open 9am–1pm Wed & Sun; call to book on other days

A monumental complex dating back to the Romans encloses the remains of a lavish bathhouse, which a few centuries later became a Byzantine church. Look out for frescoes.

3 Roman Odeon, Taormina
MAP H3 ▪ Opposite Palazzo Corvaja

Not as famous as the Teatro Antico, the Roman Odeon is still a great spot to visit. Discovered by chance in 1893, it dates back to the Octavian era and was built on the remains of a temple.

4 The White Cliffs of Sicily
On the southern coast between Realmonte and Porto Empedocle, the limestone cliffs have been shaped into steps by the elements. Known as La Scala dei Turchi, they are a popular seaside destination.

Fine-looking Villino Florio

5 Villino Florio, Palermo
MAP J3 ▪ 38 Viale Regina Margherita ▪ 091 7025471 ▪ Open 9am–1pm Tue–Sat

Villino Florio, a testament to the city's Belle Epoque era, had its interior destroyed by a fire. It is now restored to its original splendour.

6 Caravaggio in Syracuse
MAP H5 ▪ Santa Lucia alla Badia (Piazza Duomo) ▪ Open 11am–4pm Tue–Sun

This Baroque church holds one of Caravaggio's greatest and largest works, *The Burial of St Lucy* (1608).

White cliffs of La Scala dei Turchi

7 Museo della Manna, Pollina

MAP E2 ■ Piazza Duomo ■ Open 10am–1pm daily & 4pm–7:30pm Thu–Sun

This museum is in the heart of the Madonie Mountains, where manna (a natural sweetener) is harvested from ash trees. It pays tribute to this centuries-old tradition and offers an insight into local farming and agricultural traditions.

8 Regional sights and museums, first Sunday of each month

The Greek Theatre at Syracuse, the Valle dei Templi in Agrigento and Palazzo Abatellis in Palermo are some of the sights that are free on the first Sunday of each month. Many municipal and local museums are free every day to under 18s and over 65s; always ask before entering.

Valley of the Temples, Agrigento

9 Museo Archeologico Regionale, Licata

MAP E5 ■ Via Dante 12 ■ 092 2772 602 ■ Open 9am–1pm Tue–Sat, 4–6pm Thu & Sat

This small yet impressive museum houses artifacts dating back to prehistoric times, as well as a rich collection of local Greek and Roman finds. Keep an eye out for the Greek-era steel-and-gold jewellery.

10 Sagre (food festivals)

Most towns hold an annual *sagra* – a celebration of speciality food, which is a great opportunity to mix with the locals. Try Palermo and Bronte *(see p87)*.

TOP 10 BUDGET TIPS

Ferry from Panarea Island

1 Take ferries instead of hydrofoils
Ferries are cheaper than the faster hydrofoils, and you can sit outside to take in the spectacular views.

2 Buy a day pass for the bus
A €3.50 *giornaliero* ticket allows travel on buses until midnight, including the 389 to Monreale.

3 Half-price admission tickets
A full-price admission ticket can often allow half-price entry to other places. Always ask if a site belongs to an association of museums.

4 Aperitivo rinforzato
These nightly happy hours offer buffet food with your drink. Plates of seafood, pasta and cured meats can substitute for dinner – at a fraction of the price.

5 Hire a bicycle in Palermo
The city's bike-sharing programme allows visitors to get around town and travel in areas closed to traffic. Drop-off points in 50 places (www.amat-pa.it).

6 Hop-on, hop-off tour buses
A hop-on, hop-off bus tour offers a cost-effective way to see as many sites as possible.

7 Buy produce at outdoor markets
Avoid supermarkets, where possible, and shop at the markets as the locals do.

8 Drink house wine
Ask for a carafe of *vino della casa* (house wine) instead of a whole bottle.

9 Street food
Staples such as *panelle* (chickpea fritters) and *arancini* (rice balls) are fast food in Sicily, with generous portions that end up being an entire meal.

10 Return long-distance bus tickets
Buy a return ticket for long-distance buses, as these are often discounted.

TOP 10 **Feasts and Processions**

Crowds at the festival of Sant'Agata, Catania

1 Sant'Agata, Catania
Early Feb

One of the earliest saints, Agata was martyred in Catania's Piazza Stesicoro. The bejewelled reliquary bust of the saint is paraded around town followed by fanciful golden "candlesticks" so large that each one is hauled on the backs of 10 men. Balconies are draped in fabrics, flags fly, candles burn and fireworks blast at dawn.

2 Carnevale, Sciacca, Termini Imerese, Acireale
Feb

The narrow streets of these towns are packed with revellers for parades, parties and competitions. Papier-mâché floats satirize current events or figures of popular culture.

3 San Giuseppe, Belice Valley
18–19 Mar

St Joseph's Day is celebrated fervently in the west, especially in villages such as Salemi and Poggioreale. Altars are constructed in homes, schools and public spaces, piled high with ornate breads and traditional foods – but no meat, out of respect for St Joseph's poverty.

4 Good Friday, Noto
Mar/Apr

The Holy Thorn is processed through the streets accompanied by the black-veiled Grieving Madonna, whilst a drum keeps a somber tempo and a trumpet lets out a mournful blast.

5 Good Friday, Trapani
Mar/Apr

A solemn procession depicting the Passion of Christ. Tableaus are decorated with flowers and bands play funeral dirges in the streets.

Good Friday procession, Trapani

6 Easter Sunday, Castelvetrano
Mar/Apr

On Easter Sunday in Castelvetrano a celebration of Christ's Resurrection takes place in Piazza Carlo d'Aragona. The Festa dell'Aurora (Feast of Dawn) draws crowds to watch the statue of Mary, dressed in a black cape of grief, enter the square from one side, while Christ, wearing white, enters from the other. To a dramatic drumbeat, the two come together. Mary's black cape falls away to reveal a bright dress, music plays and everyone cheers.

7 Santa Rosalia, Palermo
Mid-Jul

For six days the relics of Rosalia, which are said to have saved Palermo from the plague in 1624, are paraded around the streets on top of an ornate *vera* (float).

Celebrations in Palazzolo Acreide

8 San Sebastiano and San Paolo, Palazzolo Acreide
San Paolo: 29 Jun; San Sebastiano: 10 Aug

The landowners and farmers loyal to San Paolo and the merchants and artisans loyal to San Sebastiano try to out-celebrate each other with huge statues of the saints. Worshippers process barefoot well into the night.

9 Festival of the Assumption, Randazzo
15 Aug

One of the most spectacular floats of all is paraded from Piazza di Santa Maria through the narrow streets to Piazza Loreto. The tall float carries young local boys dressed as angels, saints, Jesus and the Madonna.

10 Santa Lucia, Syracuse
Mid-Dec

A silver statue of Syracuse's patron saint travels from the Duomo to the Chiesa di Santa Lucia, while the faithful attach votive eyes to her image.

TOP 10 FOOD FESTIVALS ACROSS SICILY

1 Festival di Cannolo, Palermo
Late Apr
The art and tradition of the *cannolo* is celebrated at San Lorenzo market.

2 Sagra del Carciofo, Cerda
25 Apr
Artichoke festival; music in the piazza.

3 Mostra dei Formaggi della Valle del Belice e Sagra della Ricotta, Poggioreale
Late May or early Jun
Watch ricotta made in traditional and modern methods.

4 Festa della Ciliegia, Chiusa Sclafani
1st or 2nd Sun in Jun
Cherry festival; traditional folk music.

5 Inycon, Menfi
Late Jun–early Jul
Wine festival with food, music, dance and crafts.

6 Sagra delle Sarde, Selinunte
Late Aug–early Sep
A procession of the Madonna of the Fishermen and a sardine feast.

7 Couscous Fest, San Vito lo Capo
Last week in Sep
Chefs compete in an international couscous contest, with tastings.

8 Sagra del Pistacchio, Bronte
Late Sep–early Oct
A lively week-long festival dedicated to the tasty local nut.

9 Sagra della Cipolla, Giarratana
Mid-Aug
Savour dishes made with local flat, sweet onions.

10 Ottobrata Zafferanese
Every Sun in Oct
All over Zafferana Etnea, a fair of local wine, chestnuts, cheese and honey.

Couscous festival

Sicily
Area by Area

Picturesque resort of Cefalù

🔟 Palermo

Settled by the Phoenicians in the 8th century BC, Palermo fell first to the Romans, then to the Arab invaders, who chose Palermo for their capital, making the city one of the most magnificent and powerful in the world. This splendour was compounded during the Norman reign, which brought a western influence to the island. Today the remains of earlier ages coexist with each other and with modern life: laundry billows off balconies of 15th-century palaces; buses rumble past even older buildings displaying a mix of east and west. Buildings destroyed in World War II have been left open to the sky, but Sicilians are ever resourceful: restaurants seat diners in crumbling, yet romantic courtyards, while a once-dilapidated church has a new role as an atmospheric arts venue.

Ancient Greek terracotta vessel

PALERMO

1 Palazzo Abatellis

MAP P4 ▪ Via Alloro 4 ▪ Open 9am–6:30pm Tue–Fri, 9am–1pm Sat, Sun & hols ▪ Adm

Sicily's regional fine arts museum is housed in the 15th-century palace of a Spanish official. Highlights include a 15th-century fresco of the *Triumph of Death* (see p50).

2 San Domenico Church, Oratorio del Rosario and the Vucciria

MAP M3 ▪ Church of San Domenico: Piazza S Domenico; open 9am–1pm Mon–Sat; adm ▪ Oratorio del Rosario: Via dei Bambinai; open 9am–12:30pm Mon–Sat

Bordering the Vucciria market (see p83) to the north is the Church of San

Church and piazza of San Domenico

Domenico, burial place of notable Sicilians (see p46). Rebuilt in the Baroque style in 1640, the façade is 18th century. Behind the church is a Baroque chapel, the Oratorio del Rosario, with an altarpiece by Anthony Van Dyck.

3 La Martorana and San Cataldo

MAP L5 ▪ Piazza Bellini 3 ▪ La Martorana: open 8:30am–1pm & 3:30–5:30pm Mon–Sat, 9–10:30am Sun & hols ▪ San Cataldo: open 9:30am–12:30pm & 3–6pm daily

In Piazza Bellini there are two splendid churches. The little mid-12th-century San Cataldo has three Arab-style, bulbous red domes in a row, latticed windows and an elegant, bare interior. La Martorana has a Norman bell tower (c 1140), a 16th-century Baroque façade and original mosaic decoration (see p46).

Ceiling of La Martorana

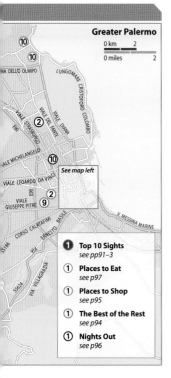

Greater Palermo

0 km   2
0 miles   2

⑩
⑩ VIA DELLO OLIMPO   LUNGOMARE CRISTOFORO COLOMBO
VIALE STRASBURGO   VIALE DELLA LIBERTÀ   VIALE DIANA
② E90
VIALE MICHELANGELO   ⑩
See map left
VIALE LEONARDO DA VINCI   E90   ②
VIALE GIUSEPPE PITRÉ   ⑨ ②
CORSO CALATAFIMI   VIALE ERNESTO BASILE   V. MESSINA MARINE
SS186
SS624   VIA VILLAGRAZIA

The New City
MAP J1

The wide, tree-lined boulevard Via della Libertà travels west from the Teatro Politeama, where the modern city begins, full of shops and cafés. It passes the Giardino Inglese, laid out with palms, to Piazza Vittorio Veneto and Royal Park (La Favorita), once a royal hunting ground.

Albergheria
MAP K6 & L6

Bordered by Via Vittorio Emanuele and Via Maqueda, this rather run-down residential area is a maze of streets strung with billowing laundry. The heart of the neighbourhood is the Ballarò market (see p83). Don't miss the 17th-century Chiesa del Carmine on Via Giovanni Grasso, with its stuccoed interior and frilly, polychrome cupola.

6 Museo Archeologico Regionale Antonio Salinas
MAP L3 ▪ Piazza Olivella 24 ▪ Open 9:30am–6:30pm Tue–Sat, 9:30am–1:30pm Sun & public hols ▪ Adm

The museum displays finds from western Sicily, from the Neolithic age to the Roman period. Among Punic and Egyptian objects is the Palermo Stone (c 2700 BC), with a hieroglyphic inscription. There are also Greek vases, Roman sculpture, and Archaic and Classical metopes recovered from Selinunte (see pp36–7).

7 Quattro Canti
MAP L5

The heart of town is the intersection of Via Maqueda and Via Vittorio Emanuele. Called the Quattro Canti (the four corners that divide Palermo into quadrants), each is swathed in sculptural decoration. The town hall is in the Piazza Pretoria, although the square is more commonly known as the Piazza della Vergogna (Square of Shame), after the shameless nudes perched around the edge of the elaborate fountain, originally intended for a Florentine garden.

Boats moored at La Cala harbour

8 La Cala and Piazza Marina
MAP N3

Yachts bobbing in the small port of La Cala can be seen from the 15th-century church of Santa Maria della Catena, while palaces line the Piazza Marina. In the centre of the lovely gardens is a statue of Garibaldi (see p43). The 1582 Porta Felice leads out to the Foro Italico and the seafront, for good waterside walks.

Palermo Cathedral displays elements of its Norman past

THE MAFIA

During centuries of absentee sovereign power, Sicilians distrusted government, built a loyalty to their own *(la cosa nostra)* and relied on justice given out by local bosses. After Unification (1860) landowners used thugs for protection and the underworld system thrived. Using crime to create fear and form alliances, the Mafia infiltrated society.

9 La Kalsa

MAP N5 ■ Bordered by Foro Italico, Via Lincoln, Garibaldi & Alloro

La Kalsa is the northeast quadrant of old Palermo, where the Arab population established their government offices. It was heavily bombed during World War II, but the once-derelict area has been gentrified in recent years. There are jewels to be discovered on nearly every corner: look out for the decadent Rococco-style Oratorio di San Lorenzo; the awe-inspiring and imposing Norman church La Magione, the former headquarters of the Teutonic knights; and the Catalan-Gothic Santa Maria della Catena church.

10 Norman Palermo

The splendid Norman kingdom in Sicily was marked by an exotic mix of cultures which is manifested in the buildings dating from the era *(see pp12–13)*. Palermo became a fine example of the best Norman architecture and decoration. Seek out the Palazzo dei Normanni and the Cathedral, which combine western and Arabic styles.

A MORNING IN LA KALSA AND ALBERGHERIA

From **Via Maqueda** take the **Piazza Santissimi Quaranta Martiri** up to the **Chiesa del Gesù** for a look at the wild Baroque decoration of the interior. Beyond the church, enter the streets taken over by **Ballarò market** *(see p83)* and spend some time weaving your way through the overloaded stalls. For a late breakfast, stop at one of the stalls serving *panelle (see p77)* or fried aubergine (eggplant) sandwiches.

From Piazza Ballarò, pass through the old neighbourhood and by the **Chiesa del Carmine**, with its colourful dome, and take the Via Case Nuove to Via Maqueda. Head into **La Kalsa** on Via Gorizia to **Via Garibaldi 43**, where you can still see parts of the magnificent original structure of the **Palazzo Ajutamicristo**. Continue past to **Santa Maria dello Spasimo** *(see p96)*, where there may be contemporary art on view. Take the residential Via della Vetreria to Via Alloro and the regional fine arts museum in **Palazzo Abatellis** *(see p91)* designed by Matteo Carnalivari.

Go south on Via Alloro until the **Piazza d'Aragona** and take a right turn into **Via A Paternostro** to the Piazza San Francesco. Have lunch at the **Antica Focacceria** *(see p97)*, sitting in the piazza under the Gothic façade of San Francesco, or in the marble and wrought-iron interior, where you can watch the chefs serving up Sicilian specialities such as *caponata (see p76)*. For dessert, there's always good *gelato* to be found at one of the *gelaterie* in the piazza.

See map on pp90–91

The Best of the Rest

1 Porta Nuova
MAP J6

This imposing gateway to the city was erected in 1569 as a triumphal arch to commemorate Charles V's victory in Tunis.

Façade of the Porta Nuova

2 Castello della Zisa
MAP D2 ▪ Piazza Zisa 1 ▪ Open 9am–6:30pm Mon–Sat, 9am–1pm Sun & hols ▪ Adm

The palace has stalactite-style ceilings, interior fountains, mosaic decoration and a collection of Arab art.

3 Palazzo Mirto
MAP N4 ▪ Via Merlo 2 ▪ Open 9am–6:30pm Tue–Sat, 9am–1pm Sun ▪ Adm

One of the few surviving aristocratic *palazzi* in Palermo. The lavish interior has 18th- and 19th-century furnishings and allegorical frescoes.

4 Oratorio di Santa Zita
MAP M3 ▪ Via Valverde 3 ▪ 091 332779 ▪ Open Apr–Oct: 9am–6pm Mon–Fri, 9am–3pm Sat; Nov–Mar: 9am–6pm Mon–Sat ▪ Adm

The interior of this chapel is covered with stucco decoration and Giacomo Serpotta's masterpiece (c 1600).

5 Palazzo Belmonte Riso
MAP L5 ▪ Via Vittorio Emanuele 365 ▪ Open 10am–7:30pm Tue, Wed & Sun, 10am–11:30pm Thu–Sat ▪ Adm

The Museum of Modern Art exhibits international and Sicilian artists here.

6 Galleria d'Arte Moderna
MAP M5 ▪ Via Sant'Anna 21 ▪ Open 9:30am–6:30pm Tue–Sun

Contemporary international art in a splendid convent.

7 Museo Internazionale delle Marionette Antonio Pasqualino
MAP P4 ▪ Piazzatta A Pasqualino 5 ▪ Open 10am–2pm Mon & Sun, 10am–6pm Tue–Sat ▪ Adm

An extensive collection of worldwide puppet traditions (see pp68–9).

8 Museo di Zoologia P Doderlein
MAP P6 ▪ Via Archirafi 16 ▪ 091 23891819 ▪ Open 9am–1pm Mon–Fri, 10am–5pm Sat ▪ Adm

Discover Sicily's diverse animals and learn about evolution at this museum.

9 Cappuccini Catacombs
MAP D2 ▪ Piazza Cappuccini 1 ▪ Open 9am–1pm, 3–6pm daily (closed Sun pm Nov–Mar) ▪ Adm

Burial site of Palermo's upper classes (1599–1881).

10 Mondello
MAP D2

This fishing village became a trendy resort in the 19th century (see p60).

View of Mondello's port

Places to Shop

1 Via della Libertà
MAP J1

Upscale Italian chains line the boulevard between the Teatro Politeama and Piazza Crispi: try Frette (No. 36) for linens, Furla (No. 14) for leather goods, Michael Kors (No. 35) for luxury accessories and Max Mara (No. 16/a) for women's fashions.

2 Via Enrico Parisi
MAP J1

For menswear, step just off Via della Libertà to find high fashion at Uomo Store (No. 21/c) and chic boutiques such as Visiona Uomo (No. 17/10). Afterwards, stop in at the equally chic Il Baretto, round the corner on Via XX Settembre 43, for an *aperitivo*.

3 Ceramiche De Simone
MAP L3 ▪ Via Cavour 38

The de Simone family has been producing high-quality hand-painted ceramics for generations, with designs of jolly Sicilian farmers and fishermen.

4 La Coppola Storta
MAP L3 ▪ Via Bara all'Olivella 72

The traditional Sicilian cap has been given a new lease of life thanks to this innovative store. All sorts of hats are available.

Sicilian caps for sale at La Coppola Storta

5 Rinascente
MAP M4 ▪ Via Roma 289

Italy's most upmarket department store has an outlet on this busy shopping street. There's a good selection of Italian *haute couture* and accessories, and a particularly good houseware department.

6 Enoteca Picone
MAP J1 ▪ Via Marconi 36

As well as over 7,000 different beverages, you'll find olive oil and cheeses *(see p83)*.

Shopping in Palermo's markets

7 Markets

Some of the best shopping in Palermo happens at the three daily food markets. They are well worth visiting even if you don't intend to buy anything *(see p83)*.

8 Punto Pizzo Free, L'Emporio
MAP M4 ▪ Via Vittorio Emanuele 172

The traditional products sold here come from various boutiques around the city, the owners of which have courageously refused to pay the *pizzo*, or Mafia protection money *(see p83)*.

9 Vincenzo Argento
MAP L5 ▪ Via Vittorio Emanuele 445

For four generations the Argento family has been practising the art of puppetry. They make traditional puppets in the Palermitan style *(see p68)* for sale and to use in rousing shows in their nearby theatre *(see p69)*.

10 Franco Bertolino
MAP K5 ▪ Salita Artale 8, corner Piazza Settangeli

Hand-painted *carrettini*, traditional Sicilian miniature carts, are sold here along with beautifully crafted papier-mâché figures and fruit.

See map on pp90–91

Nights Out

Impressive Teatro Massimo

Teatro Massimo
MAP K3 ■ Piazza Verdi ■ Guided tours ■ www.teatromassimo.it

Palermo's historic theatre reopened in 1997 after a major restoration effort. It stages lyrical opera, ballet and symphonic concerts.

Teatro di Verdura
MAP N1 ■ Viale del Fante 70

Opera, ballet, concerts and plays are presented in summer in this outdoor theatre in the garden of the former villa of the Prince of Castelnuovo.

Teatro Politeama Garibaldi
MAP K2 ■ Piazza Ruggero Settimo ■ 091 6072511/2532

This Neo-Classical theatre was opened in 1874. The season offers symphonic concerts and ballet.

Teatro Biondo Stabile
MAP L4 ■ Via Roma 258 ■ 091 7434341

Founded by the Biondo brothers as a centre for experimental theatre.

Santa Maria dello Spasimo
MAP P5 ■ Via dello Spasimo ■ 091 6161486 ■ Open 9:30am–6:30pm Tue–Sun ■ Adm

Lo Spasimo is a bombed-out church that acts as an amazing venue for an art gallery and a full programme of films and concerts (classical, contemporary, jazz), romantically staged in the roofless nave and garden space.

Associazione Culturale Palab
MAP K6 ■ Via Fondaco Palazzo Reale 5 ■ 091 6515527 ■ www.palab.it

A combination of cultural centre, theatre, music and comedy club, cinema, cocktail bar, pizzeria and restaurant, this place is always bustling with activity.

Via dei Chiavettieri
MAP M4

This pedestrian street is buzzing well into the early hours of the morning. It is lined with clubs and pubs, many with outside tables and live music.

Teatro Co-Op Agricantus
MAP J1 ■ Via XX Settembre 82/a ■ 091 309636 ■ www.agricantus.org

Agricantus is a performing arts co-op staging high-quality theatre and music, particularly for children.

Piazza Olivella
MAP L3

At night the piazza between Teatro Massimo and Via Cavour fills up with university students hanging out in the many bars lining the square.

La Cuba
MAP N2 ■ Via Sperlinga, Viale Francesco Scaduto 12 ■ 091 300846

This multipurpose venue in the beautiful Villa Sperlinga, a little way out of central Palermo, draws a smart crowd with good food, drinks and a programme of live music and DJs.

Places to Eat

1 Cin Cin

MAP K1 ■ **Via Manin 22**
■ 091 6124095 ■ Closed Sun ■ €€

Tucked away on a side street, the Italian-American Vincenzo melds traditional Sicilian with a touch of the American South. Creative cuisine.

2 Piccolo Napoli

MAP K2 ■ **Piazzetta Mulino a Vento 4** ■ 091 320431 ■ Closed Sun ■ €€

Try the pasta with lobster or any fish dish at this family-run trattoria in the little market square behind the Teatro Politeama Garibaldi *(see p78)*.

3 Osteria Mercede

MAP K3 ■ **Via Pignatelli Aragona 52** ■ 091 332243
■ Closed Mon & Tue lunch ■ €

Near Teatro Massimo, this small place serves delectable fish dishes that marry tradition and innovation. The chalkboard menu changes daily according to the catch.

Airy interior of Antica Focacceria

4 Antica Focacceria

MAP M4 ■ **Via A Paternostro 58 (Piazza S Francesco)** ■ 091 320264
■ Closed mid-Jan ■ €

Palermitan fast food and main courses under the façade of San Francesco. Sandwiches, *panelle* (*see p77*), focaccia and pasta.

PRICE CATEGORIES

For a three-course meal for one with half a bottle of wine (or equivalent meal), taxes and extra charges.

€ under €35 €€ €35–€70 €€€ over €70

---

5 Lilla e Totuccio

MAP L3 ■ **Via Bara all'Olivella 91**
■ 320 292 6255 ■ No credit cards ■ €

This street-food eatery frequented by young *Palermitani* offers a buffet of simple, tasty food, including pasta dishes. Even with wine, it's a bargain.

6 Ferro di Cavallo

MAP L4 ■ **Via Venezia 20**
■ 091 331835 ■ Closed Sun ■ €

Join the locals at this casual trattoria not far from the Quattro Canti for traditional fare and fantastic people-watching opportunites.

7 Freschette

MAP L3 ■ **Piazzetta Monteleone 5** ■ 091 9820727
■ Closed Mon ■ €

An organic, vegetarian café and market with plenty of local produce for sale and on the menu.

8 Zia Pina

MAP M4 ■ **Via Cassari 69**
■ 331 981 4546 ■ €

There may be brusque service and shabby decor at Zia Pina, but it serves arguably the best seafood in town, and at a bargain price.

9 Osteria dei Vespri

MAP M5 ■ **Piazza Croce dei Vespri 6** ■ 091 6171631
■ Closed Sun ■ €€€

A chic spot in a *palazzo* used in Visconti's film *The Leopard*.

10 Bye Bye Blues

MAP D2 ■ **Via del Garofolo 23, Mondello** ■ 091 6841415
■ Closed Mon ■ €€€

Excellent Sicilian ingredients are chosen for inventive dishes at this Michelin-starred eatery.

See map on pp90–91

📟 Northwest Sicily

Much of this area was inaccessible until relatively recently and presents unique opportunities to wander through fishing villages, watch shepherds at work and witness a way of life that has survived for centuries. The coast and offshore islands are pristine, while the mountainous interior has some of the harshest terrain in Sicily. Farmers still use mules in their fields, though younger generations are developing vineyards to produce high-quality Sicilian wines.

Blue waters and rocky cliffs of the Egadi Islands

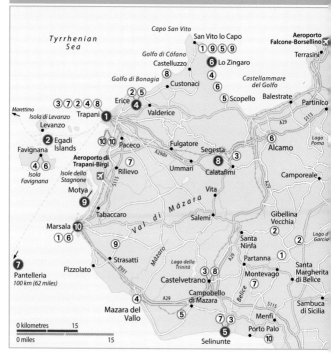

NORTHWEST SICILY

1 Trapani
MAP B2

A busy port since Spanish rule, Trapani is still a bustling place. The modern town has grown but the quaint and lively historic centre is on the tiny peninsula – the area covers less than 2.5 sq km. The main streets are lined with a mix of Baroque buildings, shops and cafés: Via Torrearsa leads from the port to the market square with its lovely loggia, and the Corso leads to the tip of the peninsula, with glimpses of everyday Sicilian life in the side streets.

2 Egadi Islands
MAP A3
■ Hydrofoil and ferry: Trapani

Levanzo, Favignana and Marettimo can be reached from Trapani in as little as 20 minutes by hydrofoil and are great for relaxing on a summer's day, as there is pretty much nothing here except for the sea. They are most famous for the *mattanza*, the Arabic tuna-fishing ritual that is still practised here in spring. Favignana is dotted with tufa quarries that give the island a pockmarked look; the caves of Levanzo's interior have Paleolithic and Neolithic paintings, and the swimming is good on all three islands. Marettimo, the furthest from the mainland (an hour from Trapani), is known for its extraordinarily clear waters.

Interior of Monreale Cathedral

3 Monreale

On this royal hill *(mons reale)* Sicily's Norman king, William II, built the mosaic-encrusted monastery and cathedral that proved to be the last and most splendid of the island's Norman monuments *(see pp14–15)*.

4 Erice
MAP B2 ■ www.funiviaerice.it

On top of a cliff above Trapani, ancient Eryx was known for its temple to Venus Erycina, so large that it served as a beacon to sailors at sea. The temple was replaced with a castle in the Middle Ages, and the village still has a medieval look. The main industry here is tourism: local artisans make good ceramics and rugs, and the views are spectacular.

5 Selinunte

The ruins of this Greek city, including temples, walls, market-place and homes, stand majestically backed by the sea – silent reminders of the glory of the once great city (see pp36–9).

Reserva Naturale dello Zingaro

6 Lo Zingaro
MAP B2

Sicily's first nature reserve was instituted in 1980 to protect 7 km (4 miles) of rocky coastline on the Tyrrhenian Sea between Scopello and San Vito lo Capo. Marked trails of various levels of difficulty traverse the steep interior, or creep along the cliff above the sea, occasionally forking down to small coves with pebble beaches. The reserve protects flora and fauna such as wild

orchids, limonium, wild carnations, dwarf palms, iris, once-widespread ilex and cork-oak forests, lichens and ferns, Bonelli's eagles, Sicilian warblers, peregrine falcons, owls, porcupines and foxes.

7 Pantelleria
MAP A6 ▪ Hydrofoils: Liberty Lines 092 3873813 ▪ Flights: Palermo and Trapani

This tiny volcanic island is actually closer to Africa than Italy. The architecture reflects Arabic influences and the island is dotted with *dammusi* – low, whitewashed, domed houses. Pantelleria is renowned for its top-quality caper production and the thick and sweet *passito* wine, made from the native Zibibbo grape, which grows well despite the ever-present *scirocco* winds that blow from the sea.

8 Segesta
MAP C3 ▪ 4 km (2 miles) from Calatafimi ▪ Open Mar: 9am–6:30pm daily; Apr–Oct: 9am–7:30pm daily; Nov–Feb: 9am–5pm daily ▪ Adm

The most romantic ruins in Sicily are tucked between the green hills and rugged mountains west of Calatafimi. The temple was built in perfect, solid Doric proportions (c 420 BC) and stands isolated on a gentle slope, turning pink in the sunset. Missing *cella*, ungrooved columns and studs around the stylobate hint that it was unfinished. The theatre, high up on Monte Barbaro, is still in use (see p44).

> **MARSALA WINE**
>
> When John Woodhouse shipped local wine to Liverpool in the 18th century, conserving it with extra alcohol, he "discovered" Marsala. The product took off and along with Englishmen Ingham and Whitaker and Italian Florio, they began a business fortifying local wine. In the 20th century, industrial versions were considered cooking wine but recent products are high quality.

9 Motya
MAP B3

■ Museo Whitaker: Open Apr–Oct: 9:30am–1:30pm & 2:30–6:30pm daily; Nov–Mar: 9am–3pm daily ■ Adm

This archaeological park occupies an entire island in Lo Stagnone, the lagoon north of Marsala, where the 8th-century BC Phoenician and later Carthaginian city of Motya (Mozia in Italian) thrived.

Greek statue, Motya

Dionysus I of Syracuse destroyed it in 398 BC, leaving it in ruins. The large archaeological collections of the Museo Whitaker (former home of the English Marsala-producing family) include the striking Greek marble statue of a youth in a diaphanous pleated tunic (c 440 BC).

10 Marsala
MAP B3 ■ Museo Archeologico Baglio Anselmi: Lungomare Boéo ■ Open 9am–12:30pm Tue, Sun & public hols, 9am–5:30pm Wed–Sat ■ Adm

This sunbaked seaside town was named by the Arabs: Marsa Allah (the port of God).It is known as the landing point for Garibaldi's Redshirts *(see p43)* and for the wine named after it. The Marsala wine trade was born in the 18th century. The Baglio Anselmi is an archaeological museum housing the treasures of Marsala's Punic past.

Roman theatre, Segesta

A DAY EXPLORING TRAPANI

Torre de Ligny
Taverna Paradiso
Trapani Market
Piazza Mercato del Pesce
Perrone Ceramiche Souvenir
San Lorenzo Cathedral
Corso Vittorio Emanuele
Via Torrearsa
Erice
Egadi Islands
Church of Sant'Agostino

▶ **MORNING**

Start off your day with a visit to Trapani's colourful **market**, which is held at the port, at **Torre de Ligny**. Well-stocked vendors are happy to offer tasters of cheeses, olives and tuna to potential customers. This is a great place to pick out a few things for a picnic. Next, walk up **Corso Vittorio Emanuele** and take a look at **Perrone Ceramiche Souvenir**'s hand-crafted ceramic pieces *(see p104)*.

Going down Corso Vittorio Emanuele, crane your neck to see the green majolica domes of **San Lorenzo Cathedral**, before turning off for Il Tonno in Piazza, in **Piazza Mercato del Pesce**, to top up your picnic provisions. When Corso Vittorio Emanuele runs into **Via Torrearsa**, walk a few hundred metres to the right to visit the pretty **Church of Sant'Agostino**, which has a 14th-century rose window, before passing through the arch and back onto Via Torrearsa. Stop at the end of the peninsula to enjoy your picnic lunch and the sea views.

AFTERNOON

Either spend the afternoon shopping in Trapani, or head up to **Erice**, with its superb views. Or take the hydrofoil to the **Egadi Islands** of Favignana.

Make it back to Trapani in time for the sunset to take part in the local *passeggiata*, then enjoy a wonderful fish dinner at **Taverna Paradiso** *(see p105)*. Order some *gelato* or the typical Sicilan dish cassata for dessert.

See map on pp98–9

The Best of the Rest

Baroque Villa Palagonia, Bagheria

 Bagheria
MAP D2

This village east of Palermo is now rather built up, but you can still see the elaborate Baroque villas built by Palermo's nobility, when it was all citrus groves and orchards.

 Cretto di Burri
MAP C2

Italian painter and sculptor Alberto Burri created this enormous outdoor cement sculpture in 1984. It is a sombre monument to the lives lost in Gibellina in the 1968 earthquake.

 Castelvetrano
MAP B3

The "City of Olives and Temples", known for its olive oil production, owes the Arabs its urban plan and its maze of piazzas. The bronze *Ephebus* (c 470 BC) is in the Museo Civico.

 Mazara del Vallo
MAP B3

This fishing port is home to the lovely Hellenic bronze statue of the *Satiro Danzante* ("dancing satyr"), found on the seabed by fishermen in 1997.

 Cusa Quarries
MAP B3 ■ Near Campobello di Mazara

This natural quarry for Selinunte lies amid olive trees, with tufa blocks and half-cut columns. Slaves had to haul columns 9 km (6 miles) to Selinunte.

 Alcamo
MAP C2

This village has a 14th-century castle of the Spanish Counts of Modica, who once ruled much of the region. It is best known for Bianco d'Alcamo, a white wine with DOC protection.

 Marinella di Selinunte
MAP C4

A fishing village with a great morning market and a small historic centre of fishermen's homes at the port. The boardwalk is lined with restaurants, bars and bathing establishments.

 Solunto
MAP D2

The Greek village of Solus was built on top of a Carthaginian settlement, high above the sea. Lacking natural springs, it developed a clever way to conserve water. Among the ruins are cisterns, channels and pools.

 San Vito lo Capo
MAP B2

On this dramatic promontory is a resort with a long sandy beach and a busy promenade in summer.

 **Saline, Saltpans**
MAP B2 ■ Museo del Sale: Via Chiusa, Nubia, Paceco ■ Open 9:30am–7pm daily ■ Adm

Exceptional sea salt is produced here using 16th-century windmills. Visit the Museo del Sale in Paceco *(see p66)*.

Landscape Features

1 Rolling Hillsides
MAP C3

The rolling hills of the Belice valley are planted with wheat – green in winter, gold in summer and burned black after the harvest – bordered by grapevines and olive trees.

2 Poggioreale Hill
MAP C3

On the road from the ruins of Poggioreale to the new town, a single wheat-covered hill rises up, topped with a lone wild pear tree.

3 Rugged Mountains
MAP C3

The rugged hills around Segesta, Calatafimi and Alcamo look dry and barren, but resourceful Sicilians plant them with sturdy vines, cultivating the hills as high as possible.

4 Quarries
MAP B2

The rocky mountains between Trapani, Castellamare del Golfo and San Vito lo Capo are rich in marble, but are slowly being destroyed by huge industrial quarries extracting the stone for office buildings.

5 Beaches
Long sandy beaches line the western coast of Sicily, reaching up to the huge stretch of sand at San Vito lo Capo. Pebble beaches are found to the northwest, on the coast of the Golfo di Castellammare.

Clear water and sandy beach

6 Faraglione
MAP C2

The rock towers at Scopello Tonnara jut out of the water and are circled by seagulls who nest in rock crevices.

7 Belice Valley
Near its mouth the wide, fertile Belice valley is long, low, flat and very good for farming; it's covered with a patchwork quilt of wine vineyards, olive groves, melon vines and citrus fruit trees. It is traversed by a typical Sicilian highway, raised on tall stilts.

Farmed fields on the hillsides, Belice

8 Promontories
MAP B2

The enormous rocky headlands rising up by the sea include Monte San Giuliano (with Erice on top), Monte Cofano (with spectacular bays and a great view of Erice), and Monte Monaco at San Vito lo Capo.

9 Plain
The mountains of the interior flatten as they near the sea towards Mazara, Marsala and up to Trapani on the northwest coast. The flat, sunbaked ground is fertile territory for grapes, olives and the saltpans.

10 Erosion
The Romans deforested Sicily to plant wheat. The result is almost treeless earth, mostly parched and prone to drastic run-off during rains.

See map on pp98–9

Traditional Shops

Airy interior of the Cantine Pellegrino

1 Cantine Pellegrino, Marsala

MAP B3 ■ Via del Fante 39 ■ www.carlopellegrino.it

This established Marsala family winery offers tours (in various languages) of the cellars and tastings.

2 Pasticceria Artigianale Grammatico Maria, Erice

MAP B2 ■ Via Vittorio Emanuele 14

This specialist sweet shop offers a wide range of delicious treats made according to recipes collected over the centuries by the sisters of Erice's San Carlo monastery (see p80).

3 Perrone Ceramiche Souvenir, Trapani

MAP B2 ■ Corso Vittorio Emanuele 106

In addition to ceramic plates, this family business also produces traditional figurines for nativity scenes, modelled on Sicilian peasants, and miniature terracotta replicas of traditional foods.

4 La Casa del Tonno, Favignana

MAP A3 ■ Via Roma 12 ■ www.iltonno.com

The name, the House of Tuna, says it all. In central Favignana, the location of the ancient tuna-fishing method called the *mattanza* (see p53), try this shop for canned tuna in oil and *bottarga* (dried tuna egg).

5 Altieri 1882, Erice

MAP B2 ■ Via Cordici 14

Since 1882, Altieri has been producing their own uniquely designed pieces in gold, coral and ceramic (see p82).

6 Cantine Florio, Marsala

MAP B3 ■ Via Vincenzo Florio 1 ■ www.duca.it/cantineflorio

Inside the Florio wine cellars is a nice store and a wine museum with a selection of antique tools used for winemaking.

7 Gustibus, Trapani

MAP B2 ■ Corso Garibaldi 119

A great selection of wines, liqueurs, oils, honey and handmade local products such as ceramics and jewellery made from coral and lava.

8 La Bottega del Pane Rizzo, Castelvetrano

MAP B3 ■ Via Garibaldi 85

Master baker Tommaso Rizzo uses local ingredients, natural yeast and a wood-burning oven to make the traditional *pane nero di Castelvetrano*, a tasty dark-brown bread. There are also the delicious *biscotti piccanti*, biscuits made with black pepper and anise. Other biscuits incorporate honey, sesame seeds and figs.

9 A Maidda, San Vito lo Capo

MAP B2 ■ Via Savoia 87

A nice selection of Sicilian treats and wines – but they don't come cheap.

10 Museo del Sale, Paceco

The museum store sells boxes of traditionally produced sea salt. Sea salt's rich flavour can vary, along with its saltiness, depending on the climatic conditions. The fine grain of the stone-ground salt also adds a pleasant texture to foods (see p102).

Places to Eat

① Pocho, San Vito lo Capo
MAP B2 ▪ Località Isulidda,
Makari ▪ 092 3972525 ▪ Closed Oct–
Easter ▪ €€

Dine in an eclectic dining room with
puppets hanging in the corners or on
the breezy terrace looking down at
Monte Cofano and the bay (see p79).

**② Taverna Paradiso,
Trapani**
MAP B2 ▪ Lungomare Dante Alighieri
22 ▪ 092 322303 ▪ Closed Sun ▪ €€€

Locally caught fish prepared simply
and with skill. Congenial service.

Typical seafood dish from Trapani

③ La Pineta, Selinunte
MAP B4 ▪ Via Punta Cantone
▪ 092 446820 ▪ €

Expertly prepared fresh fish served
on the beach under torchlight.

**④ Cantina Siciliana,
Trapani**
MAP B2 ▪ Via Giudecca 32 ▪ 092
328673 ▪ Closed Oct–Feb: Wed ▪ €

Chef Pino Maggiore offers traditional
fare, such as couscous and
almond pesto (see p79).

**⑤ Ristorante
La Terrazza,
Scopello**
MAP C2 ▪ Via Marco
Polo 5 ▪ 092 4541198
▪ Closed Tue & Nov
▪ €€

Fresh fish, caught for the
restaurant, and fine views.

PRICE CATEGORIES

For a three-course meal for one with half a
bottle of wine (or equivalent meal), taxes
and extra charges.
....
€ under €35   €€ €35–€70   €€€ over €70

⑥ La Bettola, Favignana
MAP A3 ▪ Via Nicotera 47
▪ 092 3921988 ▪ Closed Thu, mid-
Nov–Jan ▪ €

Just the catch of the day here and a
few vegetable dishes. A good place
when the tuna are running.

**⑦ Agriturismo Vultaggio,
Guarrato, near Trapani**
MAP B2 ▪ Contrada Misiliscemi 4
▪ 092 3864261 ▪ €€

Enjoy traditional Sicilian food at this
agritourism farm that produces its
own wine, oil and citrus fruits.

⑧ Le Vele, Trapani
MAP B2 ▪ Via Serisso 18
▪ 092 329743 ▪ Closed Mon ▪ €

Le Vele is elegant but not over the
top. As well as great pizzas, they
serve fish cooked in traditional
Trapani style, but their speciality is
patate alla vastasa, spicy potatoes
with onion and cheese.

**⑨ Bricco & Bacco,
Monreale**
MAP C2 ▪ Via Benedetto d'Acquisto
13 ▪ 091 6417773 ▪ Closed Mon
& Aug ▪ €€

The fare is inspired by the hearty
dishes of Sicily's interior. Look for
antipasti, meat (including *trippa*, or
tripe) and vegetable sides.

**⑩ Le 4 Stagioni,
Menfi**
MAP C3 ▪ Via delle
Margherite 15 ▪ 092
578447 ▪ Closed Nov–
Feb; Mar: Mon–Fri ▪ €€

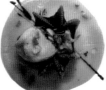

At this hotel restaurant
expect top-quality,
sea-fresh fish and
pasta dishes.

**Seafood at Le 4
Stagioni**

See map on pp98–9

🔟 Northeast Sicily

The northeast of Sicily can't help but be dominated by Mount Etna, although the region also consists of three mountain ranges, a group of islands with another active volcano, and two of Sicily's largest cities. Parts of this area have been hit by wars, earthquakes, tidal waves and lava flows, but the land and the people return from each ordeal more steadfast. Perhaps that is why feast days of the patron saints are celebrated with so much fervour. High in the Nebrodi and Madonie mountains, it seems like nothing has changed for eons – the same castles that guarded the royal paths of the interior now keep watch over the modern *autostrada*.

Crater on Vulcano Island

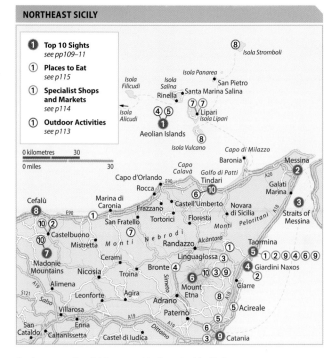

NORTHEAST SICILY

① **Top 10 Sights**
see pp109–11

① **Places to Eat**
see p115

① **Specialist Shops and Markets**
see p114

① **Outdoor Activities**
see p113

0 kilometres   30
0 miles   30

Previous pages Catania's Duomo and the Fountain of the Elephant

Aeolian Islands

The islands were declared a World Heritage Site by UNESCO in recognition of the ongoing evolution of the volcanic forms that create their spectacular scenery. The islands remain an important study area for vulcanologists (see pp16–17).

2 Messina
MAP H2

Founded by colonists from Messenia, Greece, the city grew up around the harbour. In 1908, Messina was levelled by an earthquake and tidal wave, though parts of the older city survived, including the Norman Duomo with its original portals and sculpture, a 15th-century fountain in the Piazza Duomo and a clock tower whose mechanized figures perform at noon. The Santissima Annunziata dei Catalani and the Museo Regionale, with works by Messina (see p56) and Caravaggio (see p50), also survived.

3 Straits of Messina
MAP H2

The narrow strait between Messina and Reggio di Calabria was said to be guarded by Scylla and Charybdis, mythical sea creatures who led sailors astray. A proposed suspension bridge linking Sicily and mainland Italy has been under debate for more than 30 years. Some Sicilians believe a link to the mainland would bring much-needed economic development, others fear a loss of their autonomy.

4 Giardini Naxos
MAP H3 ▪ Site and museum: Open 9am–7pm daily ▪ Adm

Naxos was founded in 734 BC, and became the first Greek settlement in Sicily. It was the setting off point for messengers taking news to Greece. The ruins, defensive walls and parts of a temple are enclosed in a park. A small museum houses local finds.

San Giuseppe church, Taormina

5 Taormina

Sicily's first true holiday resort, Taormina has been drawing visitors for centuries, all of whom fall in love with the sparkling, colourful beauty of the area (see pp18–19).

6 Mount Etna

Europe's largest active volcano dominates Sicily – from much of the island it is rarely out of sight and never out of mind (see pp20–21).

Mount Etna in the distance

Sandy beach at Cefalù

7 Madonie Mountains
MAP E3

The Madonie range, featuring Sicily's highest peaks after Mount Etna, extends from Cefalù inland and is protected by the Parco Naturale Regionale delle Madonie. The park, which encompasses spectacular countryside, includes forests of beech, chestnuts, cork oaks, poplars and fir, and tiny villages that time seems to have forgotten. The remote villages that once provided refuge to bandits on the run are now good starting points for hikes, horse riding, cycling and skiing *(see pp64–5)*.

View over the Madonie Mountains

8 Cefalù
MAP E2

This small fishing town is now a resort and must-visit area thanks to its picturesque sandy beaches and impressive cathedral *(see p47)*. Its location on a strip of land between the sea and a huge promontory looming above is also a draw. Cefalù was founded in the 4th century BC but destroyed by the Norman Count Roger in 1063. It only regained prominence thanks to his son, Roger II, who endowed the village with a bishopric and an imposing church decorated with exceptional Byzantine mosaics. The town has managed to retain its medieval character despite the arrival of modern holiday resorts. The resorts lie to either side of Cefalù because the town itself has closed its doors to the sea. It has fortified itself against storms by building tall protective stone walls, and focuses its attention inland instead.

FROM ICE TO ICE CREAM

Greeks and Romans used Mount Etna's snow to chill their wine, and the Arabs used it to make cold, sweet drinks. Sicilians were used to mixing ice, sugar and natural flavours (cinnamon, lemon, jasmine) to make granita and sorbet but by the 1700s they had perfected the craft of ice-cream-making, adding chocolate brought by the Spanish from the New World. Sicilian *gelato* is now famous the world over *(see p76)*.

Piazza Crispi

Via Bordonaro

Via Vittorio
Emanuele

Cathedral

Piazza
Marina

Piazza del
Duomo

Lavatoio

Il Normanno

Corso Ruggero

Osterio
Magno

Church of
Santa Maria
della Catena

Piazza Garibaldi

9 Catania
MAP G4

After a huge earthquake in 1693, the city was rebuilt in a unique Baroque style. The most important monuments are around the Piazza Duomo, including the Duomo itself.

Archaeological park, Tindari

10 Tindari
MAP G2

The large ruins of ancient Tyndaris, first Greek and then Roman, lie either side of the Decumanus Maximus, the main street. Homes show mosaic floors, drainage and heating systems. A restored basilica spans the street where it marked the entrance into the public area. The theatre, built by the Greeks, modified by the Romans and still in use, has views out to sea. A small museum houses finds from the site including a colossal head of Augustus. Nearby is the sanctuary of the Black Madonna.

Start your walk at **Piazza Garibaldi**, beginning at **Corso Ruggero**, where the **Church of Santa Maria della Catena** is built on top of the 4th-century BC town walls. Walking down the Corso, on the left at the corner of Via Amendola is one of the only extant parts of Norman Cefalù, besides the cathedral, the *palazzo* **Osterio Magno**. Pass the flower-filled *piazzetta* in front of the Chiesa del Purgatorio on your way to **Piazza del Duomo**, which opens up to the right. Inside the cathedral (see p47) admire the mosaics, and view the outside of the apse around the back. Sit out in the piazza at Bar Duomo with a cappuccino and enjoy the cathedral façade and the church bells marking the hour.

Continue down the Corso to the end, take a left onto **Via Bordonaro** and a right into **Piazza Crispi** with views of the Greek walls later absorbed by Spanish fortifications. Follow Via Bordonaro down to **Piazza Marina** with the small port below. Off to the left, down the **Via Vittorio Emanuele**, a staircase leads to the **lavatoio** (washbasins), the sole remnant of Arab domination.

Before lunch, wander around the "real" Cefalù, where fishermen repair boats and women pause from their laundry to chat.

Have lunch in the garden at **Il Normanno** (Via Vanni 9, close to Corso Ruggero) or pick up some picnic supplies from Alimentari e Salumeria Gatta Gaetano (Corso Ruggero 152).

See map on p108 ←

Mount Etna Eruptions

 693 BC
This massive volcanic eruption destroyed the Greek settlement at Katane (ancient Catania).

 396 BC
Lava flows from this eruption reached the Ionian Sea, preventing the Carthaginian Himilco from landing and consequently stopping him from marching on Syracuse.

 1169, 1329 and 1381
The eruptions in these three years sent lava spilling out all the way to the sea. The first caused lava to reach Aci Castello; the last flowed all the way to Catania, pouring into the sea at Ognina and covering the Portus Ulixis, which was mentioned by Virgil in the epic poem *The Aeneid*.

 1669
The worst eruption in modern times was preceded by three days of earthquakes. On the third day, a huge crevice 14 km (8.5 miles) long stretched to Nicolosi and disgorged ash, rocks and lava. The eruption lasted four months, destroying towns and leaving 27,000 people homeless.

 1886
Lava flows from this eruption once again threatened the village of Nicolosi, but the veil of St Agatha was carried in a procession and the lava miraculously stopped. It was not the first time that St Agatha had purportedly halted a lava flow.

 1911
Two major eruptions on the north side created a 5-km- (3-mile-) long crevice and 170 craters. The crevice opened up again in 1923.

7 **1928**
A huge eruption destroyed the town of Mascali, a significant amount of cultivated land and several buildings. This was the only occasion during the 20th century when a town has been destroyed.

8 **1979**
An explosion killed nine tourists who were on the edge of the main crater, then poured lava into the Valle del Bove, nearly reaching Fornazzo.

9 **1991–3**
Lava flowed down the Valle del Bove towards Zafferana Etnea; the authorities tried to divert the flow with explosives and by dropping concrete blocks from helicopters. The lava finally stopped just 1 km (half a mile) from the village.

10 **2001–2**
The most complex eruption in 300 years took place in 2001, when Etna disgorged ash and lava from six openings on the north and southeast sides, destroying the Etna Sud cable-car station. During the 2002 eruption visitors' centres and hotels were ruined, and Catania airport closed.

Plume of smoke from Mount Etna

Outdoor Activities

Alcàntara River and Gorge

1 Alcàntara Gorge
The Alcàntara River runs at the bottom of a 20-m- (65-ft-) deep basalt gorge. From the car park, with waders for hire, walk or take the lift to the bottom. You can hike between the narrow walls and over waterfalls.

2 Horse Riding, Madonie
Ranch San Guglielmo: Castelbuono; 092 1671150 ▪ Rifugio Francesco Crispi: Castelbuono; 092 1672279
The trails of the Madonie can be used by horse riders too. There are various riding stables, some are attached to good restaurants.

3 Skiing, Mount Etna
Etna Sud Ski School: 349 178 7138 ▪ Etna Nord Ski School: 347 655 1793 ▪ Etna Nord Snowboarding: 340 748 3833 ▪ www.scuolaitaliana scietna.it
There are about 10 ski runs on Etna. Lift tickets and equipment hire are available.

4 Swimming, Aeolian Islands
Good swimming abounds in the Aeolians – the water is clear and rich in marine life.

5 Boating, Aeolian Islands
The best way to visit hidden coves and grottoes, and the only way to get from island to island, is by boat. A wide selection of organized tours dock on the seven islands. Boat hire is also available.

6 Walking, Tindari
Below the promontory, from Capo Tindari towards Oliveri and Falcone, the Tindari-Oliveri reserve has quiet walks by sand formations and lakes with blue-green water.

7 Hiking, Nebrodi
The Nebrodi Mountain Park offers pastureland, yew and beech woods, birds of prey, a wetlands habitat for migratory birds, and wild horses. There are 21 villages, where artisans produce goods and food. There are marked trails for hiking.

8 Hiking, Aeolian Islands
Hike up the slopes to Vulcano's crater following the signs "al cratere". Or take a guide from the hydrofoil dock up the active volcano Stromboli.

Hiking a trail on Mount Etna

9 Hiking, Mount Etna
Gruppo Guide Alpine Etna Sud: 095 7914755; www.etnaguide.eu ▪ Gruppo Guide Alpine Etna Nord: 095 7774502; www.guidetnanord.com
Ascend to the main crater or hike the slopes accompanied by a guide.

10 Hiking, Madonie
Italian Alpine Club: 092 2057231 ▪ www.cai.it
The Madonie mountains have marked trails graded for difficulty; some are suitable for the disabled. A trail map is available. The Italian Alpine Club organizes guided tours.

See map on p108

Specialist Shops and Markets

Ceramics, Santo Stefano di Camastra

① Ceramics, Santo Stefano di Camastra
MAP F2

Shops selling Santo Stefano's famous orange-and-yellow ceramics abound.

② 'A Putia, Giardini-Naxos
MAP H3 ■ Corso Umberto 456 and Lungomare IV Novembre 249

A vast array of delicious Sicilian products, including wine, cheese, honey, pistachios and preserves. There is also a restaurant.

③ Via Etnea, Catania
MAP G4

Big-name Italian stores such as Max Mara, Benetton, Rinascente, Frette, as well as pastry shops and cafés. Emporio Armani and designer shops continue on the Corso Italia.

④ Le Colonne, Taormina
MAP H3 ■ Corso Umberto 164

The proprietor of this jewellery store in Taormina creates pieces from old stones, inspired by historical motifs; or you can create your own design (see p82).

⑤ Apicoltura Privitera, Gravina di Catania
MAP G4 ■ Via Nino Martoglio 33

Located just above Catania, this shop sells honey, wine, mead, honey vinegar, propolis and soaps.

⑥ Ceramiche dell'Artigianato Siciliano di Managò, Taormina
MAP H3 ■ Piazza San Domenico 1/2

Signor Managò's Sicilian ceramics include designs from Caltagirone and Santo Stefano di Camastra.

⑦ Fratelli Laise, Lipari
MAP G1 ■ Via Vittorio Emanuele 188

This store's booty of Aeolian goods includes capers, sundried tomatoes, honey, oregano and wine.

⑧ Markets
In villages on the slopes of Mount Etna, such as Fleri, farmers sell their produce from their trucks.

⑨ La Torinese, Taormina
MAP H3 ■ Corso Umberto 59

Since 1936, La Torinese has sold quality wines and liqueurs, tuna roe, salami, honey and olive oil.

⑩ Mount Etna Souvenirs
MAP G3

The best in lava kitsch can be found at the base of Etna Sud or Etna Nord. Ashtrays, mini statues and animal figures have been moulded from molten lava and dipped in glitter.

Souvenirs made from lava

Places to Eat

1 La Capinera, Taormina
MAP H3 ▪ Via Nazionale 177, Spisone, Taormina Mare ▪ 338 158 8013 ▪ Closed Mon ▪ €€€

Pietro d'Agostino's lovely seaside restaurant is renowned for its creative fresh fish preparations, fair prices and beautiful atmosphere.

2 Osteria Nero d'Avola, Taormina
MAP H3 ▪ Piazza San Domenico 2b ▪ 094 2628874 ▪ €€€

An "ambassador for small artisan estates", so chef Turi is called. Great atmosphere and good prices (see p79).

3 Chalet Clan dei Ragazzi, Linguaglossa
MAP G3 ▪ Pineta Ragabo ▪ 340 735 0907 ▪ No credit cards ▪ €

This rustic wooden chalet, set at 1,500 m (4,900 ft) up Etna's northern slope, serves simple, authentic food. Book in advance for dinner.

4 Pepe Rosa, Bronte
MAP G3 ▪ Corso Umberto 226 ▪ 095 7724476 ▪ Closed Mon ▪ €€

Bronte is known for its pistachios, which feature in every course at this charming little family-run restaurant. Don't miss the bruschetta with pistachio pesto.

5 La Grotta, Acireale
MAP G3 ▪ Via Scalo Grande 46, Santa Maria La Scala ▪ 095 7648153 ▪ Closed Tue ▪ €€

Bruschetta cod with olives and zucchini

Set in an actual grotto, this six-table restaurant is a local favourite thanks to top-quality fish. Booking is a must.

6 Osteria Antica Marina, Catania
MAP G4 ▪ Via Pardo 29 ▪ 095 348197 ▪ Closed Wed ▪ €€€

This osteria in the middle of the fish market sells a selection of each day's catch. Try marinated anchovies.

PRICE CATEGORIES

For a three-course meal for one with half a bottle of wine (or equivalent meal), taxes and extra charges.

€ under €35   €€ €35–€70   €€€ over €70

Dining on the Aeolian Islands

7 Ristorante Nenzyna, Lipari
MAP G1 ▪ Via Roma 4 ▪ 090 9811660 ▪ Closed Nov–Easter ▪ €

A tiny trattoria where the owner has been preparing fresh fish and other favourites for more than 40 years.

8 Trattoria da Pina, Vulcano
MAP G1 ▪ Gelso ▪ 368 668 555 ▪ No credit cards ▪ Closed mid-Oct–Easter ▪ €

Good Aeolian cuisine is served on a dockside terrace at Gelso, with views to Mount Etna.

9 Ristorante Pizzeria Granduca, Taormina
MAP H3 ▪ Corso Umberto 172 ▪ 094 224983 ▪ Closed Tue (Nov–Apr) ▪ €€

This terraced pizzeria has a garden and wonderful views.

10 Nangalarruni, Castelbuono
MAP E3 ▪ Via delle Confraternite 7 ▪ 092 1671228 ▪ Closed Wed (except Jul–mid-Sep) ▪ €€€

Great mountain food, such as pork from the Nebrodi heritage breed.

See map on p108

⊞⑩ Southwest Sicily

Beyond the beauty of the mosaics at the Villa Romana and the temples at Agrigento, sandy beaches, ruined Greek cities and olive groves feature all along the little-developed coastline of southwest Sicily. Enna dominates the wide, wheat-filled valleys, and isolated farming villages crown the hilltops, with vast expanses of rocky mountains or rolling fields in between. As a result of the lack of infrastructure and mass emigration from the region, the villages have remained almost as they were centuries ago.

Greek Temple, Agrigento

SOUTHWEST SICILY

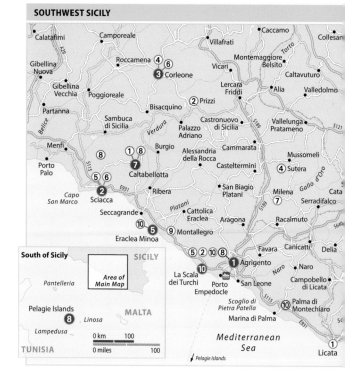

1 Agrigento and the Valle dei Templi

The Valley of the Temples was the heart of one of the most important cities in the ancient world and is a prime example of the magnificence of Magna Graecia (see pp32–5).

2 Sciacca
MAP C4

Dominated by Monte San Calogero and built on a terrace over the sea, this was the thermal spa town for Selinunte and still has a spa offering sulphur and mud baths. The small port town has a harbour with little blue-and-white boats, a thriving ceramics tradition and a good mix of old and new. Stop to admire the Porta San Salvatore

Vase from Sciacca

(1581), with its decorative reliefs, and the Catalan-Gothic Palazzo Steripinto, with its diamond-shaped rustication. Then walk down the Corso Vittorio Emanuele to the Piazza A Scandaliato for views down to the port, then on to the Duomo for its beautiful Baroque façade with Gagini sculptures.

3 Il Corleonese
MAP C3

The central zone around the village of Corleone is referred to as *il Corleonese* and has long been known for its generous water supplies and fertile soil. Remote villages are sprinkled throughout, all worth a quick visit to witness a way of life that is slow to change – visit Bisacquino, Palazzo Adriano, Cammarata, Mussomeli, Prizzi and Corleone itself, a successful modern town with a lovely historic centre.

4 Morgantina
MAP F4 ■ Open 9am–7pm daily ■ Adm

Morgantina was settled first by the Italic Morganti people, then by the Greeks in the 6th century BC, then the Romans, though it was only excavated in 1955. The large, well-preserved site comprises a split-level *agora* (forum) for town meetings, the *macellum* (covered market), large, black lava millstones, a gymnasium, a fountain with a double basin, homes with mosaic flooring, a 1,000-seat theatre and kilns for firing terracotta.

Ancient settlement of Morgantina

Madonie Mountains
Petralia Soprana
Castellana Sicula
Alimena
Suttano
Salso
Villarosa ❻❼❸❼
Santa Caterina Villarmosa ❻ Enna
❺
A19
Caltanissetta
Pietraperzia
❾❾
Morgantina ❹
Mazzarino
Aidone
Villa Romana del Casale ❾
Mmatino
San Michele di Ganzaria ❸
Riesi
Gela
Butera
Maroglio
Caltagirone
Niscemi
Falconara
Golfo di Gela Gela

0 kilometres   15
0 miles   15

Sandy beach at Eraclea Minoa

⑤ Eraclea Minoa
MAP C4 ■ Open: Apr–Sep: 9am–7pm daily; Oct–Dec: 9am–5pm daily ■ Adm

The ruins of this ancient Greek city lie on a headland above a wide sandy beach, above vineyards and olive groves and on the white sandstone cliffs. Midway between Selinunte and Agrigento and on the border between Carthaginian- and Greek-held territory, Eraclea Minoa saw its share of border disputes. Now, it is quiet and well kept. A small museum and groomed paths lead to an intimate theatre carved into the sandstone, remains of defensive walls with towers and the residential section where a few houses made of local stone have kept their floor and wall decorations. Since it's not on the standard tour bus route, the added pleasure of a visit is that you may have this place all to yourself.

View over Caltabellotta

⑥ Enna
MAP E4

Due to its easily defendable position on the top of a tall hill, Enna was almost the only town in the interior for centuries. The Greeks called it the "umbilicus of Sicily", and it was a key position for any group that wanted to take the island. Enna was so well defended that the Arabs, having tried to capture it for 20 years, resorted to crawling in through the sewer system. In the historic centre, see the Gothic Duomo with Baroque renovations and the church of San Giovanni with an Arab dome. Also visit the Museo Musical Art 3M. Once considered the geographic centre of Sicily, octagonal Frederick's Tower is 24 m (79 ft) tall and offers fine views from the top. Castello di Lombardia is a mixture of Byzantine, Arab, Norman and Swabian architecture, and is one of the largest and most important of Sicily's medieval castles *(see p48)*.

⑦ Caltabellotta
MAP C4

This tiny village, 950 m (3,100 ft) above sea level, has a lovely medieval centre. In 1090, the already fortified village was taken from the Arabs by the Norman king Count Roger, who built the Chiesa Madre and fortified the now ruined castle. It was in this castle in 1194 that William III, the heir to the Norman throne, and his mother were held prisoner and probably murdered by Emperor Henry VI; it was also the site of the signing of the 1302 peace treaty between Frederick II of Aragón and Charles of Valois, putting an end to the Sicilian Vespers *(see p42)*.

8 Pelagie Islands
MAP B6

These are three flat islands isolated in the Mediterranean. Lampione is uninhabited, Linosa has volcanic soil and clear waters. Lampedusa has constructed modern buildings for the tourist boom but it is still good for swimming, diving and watching sea turtles, dolphins and whales (in May).

Villa Romana del Casale mosaic

9 Villa Romana del Casale

The finest surviving Roman mosaics in the world cover the floors of this official's luxurious hunting villa *(see pp30–31)*.

10 La Scala dei Turchi
MAP D4

A popular summer destination for Sicilians, La Scala dei Turchi, near Realmonte, is a marl rock formation named for its natural harbour, which was a hideaway from the invading Turks in the 16th century. The ripples in the cliff, sculpted by the elements, are accessed via a limestone entrance. The well-worn path can be slippery.

ORANGES AND OTHER CITRUS FRUITS

Citrus fruits were introduced to Sicily by the Arabs and have been a cash crop for centuries. There are lemons, tangerines, mandarins and varieties of oranges, from sweet to sour, pale gold to dark purple. The plantations, around Ribera, are marked by their low-growing trees with dark-green leaves, bright fruits and heady fragrance.

AN AFTERNOON IN CALTABELLOTTA

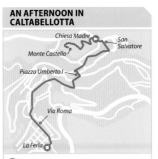

Take a late afternoon drive from the bustling town of Sciacca up to sleepy **Caltabellotta**. Skip the modern outskirts of the village to wander around the narrow streets and *piazzettas* of Terravecchia, the old medieval centre.

Terravecchia lies on a flat plain under the **Chiesa Madre**. This stark, Norman church was founded by Count Roger one year before he took Palermo *(see pp12–13)*. It has been restored, so admire the entry portal with pointed arch and the bell tower which was originally an Arabic fortification. The unornamental exterior belies the inside of this charming church where you can see the *Madonna of the Chain*, *St Benedict* and *Madonna and Child* – all works by the artist Gagini.

On the other side of the plain, opposite the Chiesa Madre, find the tiny church of **San Salvatore** with its zigzag decoration around the door.

To the north of the church, use the steps carved out of the rock to climb up to the highest point of **Monte Castello**. Walk around the ruins of Count Roger's castle, with its single Gothic doorway, and take in one of the most stunning views in Sicily. You can see the coastline to the south from Agrigento *(see pp32–5)* to Marsala *(see p101)*.

Back in Caltabellotta, stroll from **Piazza Umberto I** to **Via Roma** in the newer part of the village, where you can have an excellent dinner of traditional Sicilian mountain fare at the cosy **La Ferla** trattoria *(see p123)*.

See map on pp116–17

Chthonic Deities and their Sites

1 Demeter
The cult of the Mother Goddess, the protector of agriculture and fertility, is one of the most ancient in Sicily. When her daughter Persephone went missing, Demeter roamed the Earth searching for her, ignoring the crops and causing a famine.

Bust of Demeter dated 500–450 BC

2 Persephone
The daughter of Demeter and Zeus (also known as Kore or, to the Romans, Proserpine) rules as both queen of the underworld and goddess of fertility.

3 Persephone's Abduction
While gathering flowers with her girlfriends in fields below Enna, Persephone was abducted by Hades to reign as queen of the underworld.

Persephone returns to Earth

4 Persephone's Return
Hades freed Persephone but she had to eat a pomegranate seed, which would ensure her return to the underworld for four months a year. For four months it is winter on Earth; when she returns, it is spring.

See map on pp116–17

5 Lago di Pergusa
A deep natural lake south of Enna is the supposed site of the passage from Earth to the underworld.

6 Sanctuary at Enna
The seat of the cult of Demeter and Persephone was based at Enna on the boulder behind the castle. Their temple contained a statue of the Mother Goddess (Demeter).

7 Votive Offerings from the Sanctuary at Enna
MAP E4 ▪ Museo Archeologico, Palazzo Varisano, Piazza Mazzini ▪ Open 9am–6pm daily ▪ Adm
Items recovered from the sanctuary and from sites near Lake Pergusa are preserved in Enna's Museo Archeologico, including votive statuettes of Demeter.

8 Rock Sanctuary of Demeter, Agrigento
The Earth goddesses were venerated at a walled sanctuary in Agrigento, which is now marked by the church of San Biagio. The church was built on top of a 5th-century BC temple, of which two round altars remain.

9 Sanctuary at Morgantina
Demeter and Persephone were worshipped as the protectors of Morgantina. In the sanctuary it is possible to see purification baths, altars for performing rituals and a well for sacred offerings.

10 Sanctuary at Palma di Montechiaro
Three small 7th-century-BC votive statuettes of the goddesses Demeter or Persephone are now in the archaeological museum in Syracuse. They were recovered from the sanctuary of Palma di Montechiaro, between Agrigento and Gela.

Scenic Views

1 From Caltabellotta
MAP C4

From the ruins of the Norman castle above Caltabellotta (see pp118 and 19) you can see all the way to the flat coast towards Marsala and the hilly interior dotted with villages and farms.

2 Prizzi
MAP D3

Driving through the Corleonese zone (see p117), Prizzi is one of the highest towns, covering the top of its hill like a *coppola* (peasant farmer's cap).

3 Views from Enna
MAP E4

From the Piazza Crispi, see across the deep valley to Calascibetta on the flat top of its own terraced hill, as well as across the interior all the way to Mount Etna.

4 Sutera

Set amid the Sikanian hills, Sutera affords sweeping vistas to the Mediterranean and Mount Etna, with seemingly endless fields of wheat below. Spring is pretty when there are swathes of wildflowers such as sulla, poppies and buttercups.

5 The Valle dei Templi by Night

Agrigento's temples are romantic at night. Attractive from any vantage point, perhaps the finest view is from a restaurant's terrace, dining with the Temple of Concord as a backdrop (see pp32–5).

6 Countryside around Il Corleonese

Vast expanses of rolling terrain are planted with wheat, vines, olives and silvery blue artichokes. There are bright blankets of crimson sulla, red poppies and hearty yellow fennel growing impossibly tall (see p117).

7 Vallate near Enna
MAP E4

The enormous fertile *vallate* (valleys) around Enna are planted with wheat, and the spectacular stretches of soft golden fields change colour with the seasons, from lush green, to pale yellow, to black.

8 The Rocca di Nadore
MAP C4

The round-topped Rocca di Nadore above Sciacca turns its flat, white face towards the sea and dominates the coast for miles. See it looming on the horizon as far away as Selinunte.

9 From Morgantina

From the residential sector of the ancient site on the east hill, look down on the *agora* (forum) and out towards the east coast and the outline of Mount Etna (see p117).

10 From Eraclea Minoa

From the ruins of Eraclea Minoa on top of a striking white sandstone cliff, look down towards the wide stretch of sandy beach and the dark sea below (see p118).

Temple of Concord by night

Local Produce

Vineyards, Regaleali

1 Wine

During the 20th century large estates growing wheat and other crops also started to cultivate vines to produce high-quality wine. Two good examples are Regaleali *(see p75)* near Vallelunga and Planeta near Sambuca di Sicilia.

2 Oranges

Ribera is well known for its production of the prized Washington variety of navel orange, introduced to the area by emigrants returning from North America.

3 Co-operative Produce

In and around Corleone *(see p117)*, several co-operatives under the umbrella *Libera Terra* cultivate land confiscated from Mafia bosses to create jobs and strengthen the economy of the area. Wheat is grown for pasta, grapes for wine, as well as fruits, cheeses and honey.

4 Preserved Fish

Preserved tuna was a staple food for centuries on ships sailing the Mediterranean, and tuna as well as anchovies and sardines are still big business. At Sciacca, anchovies and sardines are processed by hand and packed under salt or olive oil for export all over the world.

5 Olive Oil

Cities such as Castelvetrano and Trapani are famous for their olives. The harvest begins in October, and first pressings of the extra virgin olive oil are available from the end of November. Towns celebrate the new season's oil with tastings.

6 Fresh Fish

Fishing villages line the southern coast of Sicily, with centres at Licata, Porto Empedocle and Sciacca.

7 Wheat

Latifondi (large estates owned by nobility) took up much of the interior until well into the 20th century. Today, vast valleys and hills are devoted to cultivating Sicily's special wheat known as *grano duro,* which is an important source of income *(see p77).*

8 Cheese

Sicily is renowned for its cheeses, made from both cow and sheep's milk. Look for the sharp Caciocavallo Ragusano, the saffron-infused Piacentino di Enna and the soft Vastedda del Belice.

9 Broad Beans

Large broad beans, or *fave,* are cultivated in the countryside near Enna. They are eaten dressed with olive oil or used in soups.

10 Artichokes

A staple of Sicilian cuisine, they are at their best in spring. Cerda has a three-day artichoke festival in April.

Artichokes for sale

Places to Eat

1. La Madia, Licata
MAP E5 ▪ Corso F Re Capriata 22 ▪ 092 2771443 ▪ Closed Tue, Sun dinner; Sun lunch (Jul & Aug) ▪ €€€

Chef Pino Cuttaia is creative and dedicated to seasonality at this small restaurant in Licata (see p79).

2. Trattoria dei Templi, Agrigento
MAP D4 ▪ Via Panoramica dei Templi 15 ▪ 092 2403110 ▪ Closed Sun ▪ €

This family-run trattoria has an excellent Sicilian menu: try pasta with swordfish and mint.

Pasta alla Norma

3. Ristorante Pomara, San Michele di Ganzaria
MAP F4 ▪ Via Vittorio Veneto 84 ▪ 093 39760976 ▪ €

The stone fireplace in this restaurant is where local cheeses, vegetables and meats are grilled for hearty dishes such as pasta with pistachios.

4. Ristorante Gennaro, Corleone
MAP C3 ▪ Corso Dei Mille 132 ▪ 091 8464767 ▪ €€

Run by a couple, this restaurant serves traditional Sicilian cuisine and pizzas, alongside artisanal craft beer.

5. Osteria il Grappolo, Sciacca
MAP C4 ▪ Via Conzo 9/A ▪ 092 585294 ▪ Closed Tue ▪ €

Sicilian dishes here are made with products from the family's small farm and the fish is fresh from the sea.

6. Porto San Paolo, Sciacca
MAP C4 ▪ Largo San Paolo 1 ▪ 092 527982 ▪ Closed Wed, mid-Oct–mid-Nov ▪ €€

The daily catch is cooked in typical Mediterranean style. Terrace tables look over Sciacca's small port and out to sea.

PRICE CATEGORIES

For a three-course meal for one with half a bottle of wine (or equivalent meal), taxes and extra charges.

€ under €35   €€ €35–70   €€€ over €70

---

7. La Lanterna, Milena
MAP D4 ▪ Via Pietro Nenni 8 ▪ 093 4933478 ▪ Closed Mon ▪ €

An informal trattoria with traditional local Sicilian food. The set menu is good value.

8. La Ferla, Caltabellotta
MAP C4 ▪ Via Roma 29 ▪ 092 5951444 ▪ Closed Mon, Oct ▪ €

A local favourite. Try the roasted artichokes and local cheeses. Sea views.

9. Capitolo Primo del Relais Briuccia, Montallegro, near Agrigento
MAP D4 ▪ Via Trieste 1 ▪ 339 759 2176 ▪ Closed Mon ▪ €€

Creative versions of Sicilian dishes with items from wild fennel to saffron.

Capitolo Primo del Relais Briuccia

10. Ruga Reali, Agrigento
MAP D4 ▪ Cortile Scribani 8 ▪ 092 220370 ▪ Closed Sun ▪ €

An informal *osteria* popular with locals and specializing in fish dishes. The 15th-century building has beams and a courtyard for alfresco dining.

See map on pp116–17

Southeast Sicily

Baroque ornamentation

The landscape of the southeast is different from the rest of the island: here the white limestone strata with scrubland is broken by steep gorges and low dry-stone walls. The Greek and Roman remains at Syracuse are spectacular, while Caltagirone, Modica, Noto, Palazzolo Acreide, Ragusa and Scicli have all been declared World Heritage Sites thanks to their Baroque architecture and urban planning. There is also a gastronomic renaissance taking place in this area. Seafood from the coastal zones, along with meat, cheese and wild greens from the interior are being used by young chefs aware that old traditions and even ingredients are on the brink of extinction. They are returning to their roots and preserving and revitalizing the authentic cuisine of the region.

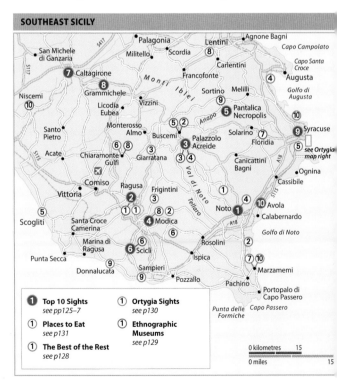

SOUTHEAST SICILY

- **1** Top 10 Sights
  see pp125–7
- **1** Places to Eat
  see p131
- **1** The Best of the Rest
  see p128
- **1** Ortygia Sights
  see p130
- **1** Ethnographic Museums
  see p129

0 kilometres   15
0 miles   15

Spectacular location of Ragusa Ibla

 Noto

Noto was rebuilt in Baroque style after the earthquake of 1693, using a tufa stone that has turned a golden shade. There are wide streets and plenty of piazzas and *piazzettas* for the *passeggiata* (see pp28–9).

 Ragusa
MAP F5

Ragusa was founded as Hybla Heraia by the Sicels. After the earthquake of 1693, half the population rebuilt on the ridge above (Ragusa) while the other half renovated the old village (Ragusa Ibla). Ibla has a dramatic location with its buildings clinging to the side of a cliff. The Duomo, a Gagliardi masterpiece, is at the heart of town, while the oval-shaped church of San Giuseppe has another striking Baroque façade.

Greek Theatre, Palazzolo Acreide

Palazzolo Acreide
MAP G5

The Baroque town was originally a Greek colony of Syracuse, founded in 664 BC. Next to the town, the small, 600-seat Greek theatre remains in good condition, although the temples to Persephone and Aphrodite are in ruins. A short walk from the old city is I Santoni, a sanctuary dedicated to the fertility goddess Cybele (see p58).

4 Modica
MAP G6

Rebuilt after 1693, on and between two deep gorges, the city is divided in two parts – Modica Alta, the upper town, and Modica Bassa, the lower town. Founded by the Sicels, the city fell under Spanish rule, when it was the capital of a quasi-autonomous state ruled by Spanish barons. The lively Corso Umberto I, with cafés, boutiques, pastry shops, numerous palaces and a theatre, crosses Modica Bassa. Also on this street is a monumental flight of steps with fine Baroque statues of the Apostles that leads up to the post-1693 church dedicated to San Pietro. Up the hill, Modica Alta's Baroque Duomo di San Giorgio is attributed to Gagliardi.

Pantalica Necropolis

5 Pantalica Necropolis
MAP G5

Pantalica was at the heart of ancient Hybla (known through its striking red-glazed pottery, examples of which are on view in Syracuse). The Anapo River carved a gorge through the limestone, creating what became Sicily's largest necropolis; there are more than 8,000 tombs here. A hike through the gorge takes you past thousands of burial sites, carved into the cliff sides, as well as remains of a medieval settlement, wild orchids, rabbits, porcupines and falcons.

6 Scicli
MAP F6

Dominated by a high, rocky cliff, Scicli was an outpost of the Spanish barons during their long reign over the County of Modica. From the wide

CAROB TREES

Huge *carrubi* (carob trees) are a feature of southeast Sicily. The trees produce a fruit shaped like a brown pea pod, with sweet flesh and small, hard seeds. The seeds are amazingly uniform and were the original carat used to weigh precious stones. Carob's sweet flesh can be used in pasta and sweets. Once called "poor man's chocolate", the deep, rich flavour is now prized by chefs.

Piazza Italia, the Via Nazionale passes the street where the Palazzo Beneventano sits on a corner, its sculpture now weathered by the elements. Via Nazionale continues to Piazza Busacca, with views into the older, residential section of town, with its narrow lanes and terracotta roofs.

7 Caltagirone
MAP F4

Named after the Arabic *Cal'at Ghiran* (Castle of Vases), ceramic production has been the main industry in this town since prehistoric times (visit the local Museo della Ceramica). The Baroque town built onto the hillside is a pleasure to wander through, with alleyways, cafés and ceramics shops. A stairway leads from the lower town up to the church of Santa Maria del Monte, and each of the 142 steps is decorated with majolica tiles.

Tiled steps to Santa Maria del Monte

8 Grammichele
MAP F5

Built by the Principe di Butera after the 1693 earthquake to house the farmers of the destroyed village of Occhiolà, there is an authentic peasant-farmer feel here, though it was built on a grand plan inspired by Renaissance mathematical ideals. Concentric hexagonals radiate from around the central Piazza Umberto I, home to private residences, *palazzi*, the Chiesa Madre and the town hall.

Façade of the Cathedral, Syracuse

9 Syracuse

The remains of the mighty powerhouse of Magna Graecia make up some of the most important sites in Sicily, while the small historic centre of Ortygia *(see p130)* is one of the most pleasant town centres on the island *(see pp24–7)*.

10 Avola
MAP G5

The almond-growing capital of Italy, Avola also lends its name to one of the best-known red wines produced in Sicily. Dating back to the prehistoric Sicanian era, Avola was a predominantly Greco-Roman city and artifacts from these eras can be seen in the small Roman villa and megalithic dolmen. Facing the Ionian Sea, it is a charming town with quaint Baroque buildings and sandy beaches. Visit the Cava di Cassibile nature reserve, home to a rare species of orchid.

A DAY IN MODICA AND RAGUSA IBLA

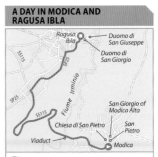

▶ MORNING

Spend a morning in **Modica** *(see p126)*, stopping by the church of **San Giorgio of Modica Alta** on your way into town. In Modica Bassa, visit the equally splendid Sicilian Baroque church of **San Pietro**. Walk down the Corso Umberto I towards Duomo di San Giorgio, passing cafés, shops and buildings that incorporate parts of pre-earthquake structures. At Corso Umberto I, 156, visit the *biscottificio* of **Donna Elvira Dolceria** *(see p81)* and, at 159, Dolceria Bonajuto, the oldest chocolate factory in Sicily, to taste and buy a wide range of Modica's traditional sweets.

Drive along the SS 115 to **Ragusa** *(see p125)*. On the way, you will cross a **viaduct**, which is one of the tallest of its kind in Europe, before travelling into a fertile land of citrus groves and carob trees. In Giardini Iblei park, pick up a map of the maze-like streets from the information office. Next door, have lunch at **Ristorante Duomo** *(see p131)*.

AFTERNOON

Spend the afternoon wandering through Ragusa Ibla to see the Duomo di San Giorgio and the church of San Giuseppe. You can study the Baroque façade of the Duomo from the lively piazza with a treat from Gelati DiVini (Piazza Duomo 20) – their ice cream is made from Sicilian wines. But don't fail to walk through the narrow side streets, where tiny alleys are connected with staircases and tunnels, for a taste of authentic Ragusa Ibla.

See map on pp124–5

The Best of the Rest

Noto Antica
MAP G5

To the northwest of Noto lie the evocative ruins of the old pre-earthquake town. Built on an arid, limestone ridge, the site commands views of the Ragusan plain and Mount Etna. Under the hot Sicilian sun, purple thistle and sun-dried herbs perfume the air.

Cave homes, Noto Antica

Vendicari
MAP G6

The reserve's maquis supports thyme, rosemary and juniper; the wetlands host migratory birds. Depending on the season, watch for herons, egrets and flamingoes.

Giarratana
MAP G5

The narrow streets of this tiny town in the middle of the Monte Iblei are lined with residences, palaces and churches. The typical low doors protect against cold winter winds.

Megara Iblea
MAP G5

Lovely and extensive coastal remains of a town founded in 728 BC by Greek colonists from Megara, near Athens.

Ciane River
MAP G5

The river's source is said to be a pool formed by the tears of Cyane, who tried to prevent Persephone's abduction into the underworld. The river banks are thick with papyrus. Take a boat tour past the Olympieion.

Cave d'Ispica
MAP G6

An ancient river carved out this gorge, now an open-air park with excellent walks and climbs. The cliff sides are hollowed out to form ancient tombs of religious hermits; in one cave is a Byzantine fresco of the Madonna.

Marzamemi
MAP G6

This little fishing village grew up around the *tonnara* (tuna fishery) and villa of the noble Villadorata family. Modern resort features, including popular nightclubs, have been added.

Lentini
MAP G4

The excavations of this small, but important and powerful former Greek colony are worth exploring.

Sampieri
MAP F6

Clear waters and sandy beaches surround what was once a small fishing village. The beaches at Punta Pisciotto are accessed from a turn-off at the abandoned, temple-like brick kilns called Fornace Penna.

Castello Euríalo
MAP G5 ■ Open 9am–5:30pm daily ■ Adm

This Greek military castle was built in 402 BC and is notable for its 15-m (50-ft) keep. Enjoy views of the coast from its fortifications *(see p49)*.

Castello Euríalo fortifications

Ethnographic Museums

① Museo del Tempo Contadino, Ragusa

MAP F5 ▪ Palazzo Zacco, Via San Vito 158 ▪ Open 9am–1pm Mon, Wed & Fri, 9am–5pm Tue & Thu ▪ Adm

Palazzo Zacco houses a collection of historic farming and farm kitchen tools, lace and embroidery work.

② I Luoghi del Lavoro Contadino, Buscemi

MAP G5 ▪ Via Libertà 10 ▪ Open 9am–1pm Mon–Fri, 8am–noon Sat ▪ Adm

Buscemi is a living museum. Eight workrooms and living spaces, including the home of a peasant farmer, a smithy and a mill, have been faithfully preserved.

③ Casa-Museo di Antonino Uccello, Palazzolo Acreide

MAP G5 ▪ Via Machiavelli 19 ▪ Open 9am–7pm Mon–Sat, 2:30–7:30pm Sun ▪ Adm

Exhibits of Sicilian peasant farmers' handmade objects (see p51).

④ Mulino ad Acqua Santa Lucia, Palazzolo Acreide

MAP G5 ▪ Valle dei Mulini 10 ▪ Open 9am–1pm Mon–Sat ▪ Adm

Antique water-powered grain mill complete with working millstones.

⑤ Centro di Documentazione della Vita Popolare Iblea, Buscemi

MAP G5 ▪ Via Vittorio Emanuele ▪ Open 9am–1pm Mon–Sat ▪ Adm

The centre preserves 180 hours of film and 12,000 prints, which document agricultural life.

⑥ Museo del Costume, Scicli

MAP F6 ▪ Cortile Opera Pia Carpentiera, Via Francesco Mormina Penna 65 ▪ Open 6:30–11pm daily (also 10:30am–12:30pm Fri–Sun)

The museum is dedicated to keeping alive the history and culture of the Iblean mountain communities.

I Luoghi del Lavoro Contadino

⑦ Museo della Civiltà Contadina Iblea, Floridia

MAP G5 ▪ Piazza Umberto I, 27 ▪ Open 5:30–8:30pm Mon–Fri ▪ Adm

Mills for wheat and olives, looms and a range of tools have been collected from farmers' homes throughout the Iblean countryside.

⑧ Museo del Ricamo e dello Sfilato, Chiaramonte Gulfi

MAP F5 ▪ Via Laurea 4 ▪ Open Jun–Sep: 10am–1:30pm & 5–8:30pm Fri–Sun & public hols ▪ Adm

Antique looms and instruments for producing thread and cloth are here.

⑨ A Casa do Fascitraru, Sortino

MAP G5 ▪ Via Gioberti 5 ▪ Open by appt ▪ 093 1952992 ▪ Adm

Sortino is well known for its beekeeping tradition. This museum displays beekeeping and honey-making implements.

⑩ Museo di Civiltà Contadina Angelo Marsiano, Niscemi

MAP F5 ▪ Via Mazzini 78 ▪ Open 10am–noon, 4–6pm in summer, or on request ▪ 093 3951722

Displays on life in the Sicilian countryside and traditional crafts.

See map on pp124–5

Ortygia Sights

1 **Ortygia**
MAP H5
The tiny island is a bustling mix of temples, churches, museums, open piazzas, seaside bars, markets and shops. It is also lively after hours.

2 **Temple of Apollo**
On Largo XXV Luglio are the remains of the Doric Temple of Apollo. Built in 575 BC, this was the first temple in Sicily with an exterior stone colonnade. Two monolithic sandstone columns remain (see p25).

3 **Duomo**
One of the most spectacular buildings in Sicily, the dramatic Baroque façade fronts a 5th-century-BC Doric temple. It was transformed into a church in the 7th century AD. Clearly visible inside and out are monolithic Doric columns.

4 **Piazzetta San Rocco**
This piazza and the network of streets around it are the hub of Ortygia's nightlife.

5 **Via Maestranza**
Now lined with boutiques and restaurants, this street was where noble families built their Baroque palaces, which often incorporated older structures.

6 **Piazza del Duomo**
Excavations in this square have unearthed the remains of 8th-century-BC houses from the original Sicel culture. Around the oblong piazza are the Duomo, the town hall (located atop an Ionic Temple to Artemis) and outdoor cafés.

7 **The Greek Ghetto**
The six streets between Via della Giudecca and Via GB Alagona follow the Greek urban plan. The area is still crowded with medieval houses and laundry drying in the breeze.

8 **Fonte Aretusa**
The mythical Arethusa (see p43) was turned into a spring and bubbles up on the shores of lower Ortygia. Along the Lungomare Alfeo, a terrace looks down on the spring that now feeds into a pond, with ducks and tall papyrus.

9 **Castello Maniace**
Open 1–5:15pm Mon, 8:30am–1pm Tue, Fri & Sun, 8:30am–5:15pm Sat ▪ Adm
Frederick II built this castle around 1239. It takes its name from the Byzantine George Maniakes who "liberated" Syracuse during the 11th century.

10 **Market**
Via del Mercato & Via Trento ▪ Mon–Sat am
The market bustles with local housewives and vendors yelling out the merits of their wares. Farmers and fishermen heap tomatoes, mussels, cherries and more into colourful mounds to entice local customers.

Piazza del Duomo, Ortygia

Places to Eat

PRICE CATEGORIES
For a three-course meal for one with half a bottle of wine (or equivalent meal), taxes and extra charges.

€ under €35 €€ €35–€70 €€€ over €70

 Ristorante Duomo, Ragusa Ibla

MAP F5 ■ Via Capitano Bocchieri 31 ■ 093 2651265 ■ Closed Sun; lunch except for Mon ■ €€€

Ciccio Sultano expertly chooses local ingredients. The traditional Ragusan food is outstanding, and is served in an elegant dining room (see p78).

 Singola, Modica

MAP G6 ■ Via Risorgimento 88 ■ 093 2904807 ■ Closed Tue; Sat & Sun lunch ■ €€

Singola uses fresh ingredients in season from local farms, which are organic when possible, in its creative vegan dishes. There's also a great atmosphere here.

③ Ristorante Fidone Maria, Frigintini

MAP F5 ■ Via Gianforma 6 ■ 093 2901135 ■ No credit cards ■ Closed Mon; Sat & Sun lunch ■ €

This family-run trattoria near Ragusa prepares everything in house, and it's all excellent (see p78).

④ Ristorante Crocifisso, Noto

MAP G5 ■ Via Principe Umberto 48 ■ 093 1571151 ■ Closed Wed ■ €€

This family-run restaurant offers recipes such as coniglio stimperata (sweet-and-sour rabbit), fried ricotta, and ravioli in pork ragù.

 Sakalleo, Scoglitti

MAP F5 ■ Piazza Cavour 12 ■ 093 2871688 ■ €€

The menu depends upon what the fishing boats bring in. The animated owner may also have a glass of wine with you.

⑥ Majore, Chiaramonte Gulfi

MAP F5 ■ Via Martiri Ungheresi 12 ■ 093 2928019 ■ Closed Mon & July ■ €

"Quì si magnifica il porco" (Here the pig is glorified) is the motto of this eatery, which is also a butcher's (see p78).

Fresh fish at La Darsena da Ianuzzo

⑦ La Darsena da Ianuzzo, Syracuse

MAP H5 ■ Riva Garibaldi 6, Ortygia ■ 093 166104 ■ Closed Mon ■ €–€€

Feast on fresh fish, perfectly and traditionally cooked, in the dining room or the waterfront terrace.

⑧ Accursio, Modica

MAP G6 ■ Via Grimaldi 41 ■ 093 2941689 ■ Closed Mon ■ €€€

Michelin-starred restaurant offering creative Sicilian cuisine (see p78).

⑨ Al Molo, Donnalucata

MAP F6 ■ Via Cernia 13 ■ 093 2937710 ■ Closed Mon in winter ■ €€

Sit on a veranda facing the wharf where fishermen sell their catch. Fish is prepared simply or in more elaborate Sicilian dishes.

⑩ La Cialoma, Marzamemi

MAP G6 ■ Piazza Regina Margherita 23 ■ 093 1841772 ■ Closed Tue (Dec–May), Nov ■ €€–€€€

Enthusiastic service, a tasty, mainly fish-based menu and a great wine list are served in this romantic square with live music in summer (see p78).

See map on pp124–5

Streetsmart

Colourful traditional Sicilian
painted plates

Getting To and Around Sicily

Arriving by Air

Sicily's four international airports are situated in Catania, Palermo, Trapani and Comiso and have excellent links to the nearest city centre as well as to smaller villages. **Aeroporto di Catania-Fontanarossa** is 6 km (4 miles) from the city centre, best reached by the **Alibus** shuttle. Tickets can be bought on board. Major coach companies, including **Ast**, **Sais** and **Etnabus**, stop outside the arrivals hall and provide excellent links to out-of-town destinations. Taxis into town start at €20.

Palermo's **Aeroporto Falcone-Borsellino** is roughly 35 km (22 miles) from the city centre. The **Prestia e Comandè** bus service will take you to the centre in 30 minutes; tickets can be purchased online or on board. Taxis to the centre start at €40. Two trains run between the airport and Palermo's Stazione Centrale every hour and the journey takes 60 minutes.

The west coast of Sicily is served by **Aeroporto di Trapani-Birgi**. A regular shuttle service into the city centre is run by **Ast**, while taxis start at €30.

The southeast is served by the **Aeroporto Pio La Torre** in Comiso. Bus company **Tumino** has a service to Ragusa, with stops in towns along the way. Ast and Etnabus run a good service to other destinations in the southeast. Taxis to Ragusa start at €30. Sicily also has the **Aeroporto di Pantelleria** and the **Aeroporto di Lampedusa** serving domestic traffic.

Arriving by Rail

Trenitalia provides a rail service to all major cities in Sicily, smaller towns around the island and from mainland Italy, with an overnight service from Rome Termini to Palermo Centrale as well as to Catania Centrale.

Although trains running between the larger cities are fast, service to and from smaller towns can be painfully slow. They are, however, more comfortable than coaches, and in addition offer views of some of the prettiest landscapes in Sicily.

Before you board the train your ticket must be stamped with the time at the *obliteratrice*. These white and green machines are found on the platform or near the ticket booth. Failure to get your ticket stamped will result in a fine. If travelling on the Messina-Palermo or Syracuse-Messina lines remember to make sure that the ticket does not also require you to get a *supplemento rapido* – a surcharge that is applied to some express trains. The validity of tickets is usually two to six hours depending on the length of the journey.

Arriving by Road

If you plan to arrive by road you will need to drive your vehicle onto a ferry either at Reggio Calabria or Villa San Giovanni and disembark in Messina. Sicily has a good system of highways that reaches all the major cities; most highways are toll free. Tolls are payable on the A20 from Buonfornello to Messina, and the A18 from Messina to Catania. Driving is on the right.

In the major cities such as Palermo or Catania it is advisable to park your car in a guarded parking area with a custodian, especially if you have your belongings in the car. If you are parking your car on the street make sure that there are no parking meters for that zone, otherwise you will receive a parking fine.

Arriving by Boat

Ferry and hydrofoil services arrive at the main ports of Palermo, Catania, Messina, Trapani and Milazzo. **Siremar**, **SNAV** and **Tirrenia** manage the bulk of the services to Sicily from Naples, while **Caronte e Tourist** handles the service from Calabria. Long-distance ferry services from Civitavecchia (the port of Rome), Livorno and Genoa are operated by **Grandi Navi Veloci**, and Tirrenia and **Virtu Ferries** runs a service to Catania from Malta.

Arriving by Coach

Both Sais and Etnabus offer a long-distance bus service to Sicily from Milan, Perugia and Rome. There are stops to all major Sicilian cities and towns, but services are not always direct, so you will need to change buses once or twice along the way. Travelling by coach seems to be the preference for many Sicilians, especially commuters and students, as it connects big cities with remote towns and villages that are not served by rail. Sais and Etnabus offer a cost-effective alternative to driving, especially for day trips out of town. Unlike the rail service, they apply discounts to same-day return tickets.

Getting Around by Taxi

Taxis are almost always white with the "Taxi" sign on top. When you arrive at the airport always take a taxi from the rank and ignore shady types who shout "taxi" in your face – these are drivers without taxi licences.

Taxis are available in all airports and in city centres, but unlike New York or London, you can only hail one if you go to the nearest rank or phone one. Expect additions to the base price such as night, weekend and holiday surcharges, and per item of luggage. Always try to set the price before travelling to avoid surprises. If you prefer a set fare it is a good idea to make a booking through the designated taxi desks at arrivals.

Although tipping taxi drivers is not required, if you have received good service, you can leave a few euros or 10 per cent of the fare.

Getting Around by Scooter

A scooter offers more freedom than a car, but it can take strong nerves to drive one in cities like Palermo or Catania, with their hair-raising traffic. If you're up to it, **Rental Motor Bike** offers good deals in major cities.

Getting Around by Bicycle

BiciPa, the bike-sharing programme in Palermo, includes 50 drop-off points around the city. Bed and breakfasts often rent bikes for a small fee.

Getting Around on Foot

The best way to take in a city is usually on foot because walking provides the opportunity to discover a wealth of unexpected, hidden-away sights. However, it is also worth bearing in mind that there can be a lot of ground to cover: Palermo has a historical city centre that covers 2.5 sq km (1 sq mile), and many of the archaeological sights involve uphill climbs. Pace yourself accordingly, and wear footwear that is both sturdy and comfortable.

DIRECTORY

ARRIVING BY AIR

Aeroporto di Catania-Fontanarossa
w aeroporto.catania.it

Aeroporto Falcone-Borsellino
w gesap.it

Aeroporto di Lampedusa
w aeroportodi lampedusa.com

Aeroporto di Pantelleria
w aeroportodi pantelleria.it

Aeroporto Pio La Torre
w aeroportodicomiso.eu

Aeroporto di Trapani-Birgi
w airgest.it

Alibus
w sitabus.it

Ast
w aziendasiciliana trasporti.it

Etnabus
w etnatrasporti.it

Prestia e Comandè
w prestiaecomande.it

Sais
w saisautolinee.it

Tumino
w tuminobus.it

ARRIVING BY RAIL

Trenitalia
w Trenitalia.it

ARRIVING BY BOAT

Caronte e Tourist
w carontetourist.it

Grandi Navi Veloci
gnv.it

Siremar
w siremar.it

SNAV
w snav.it

Tirrenia
w Tirrenia.it

Virtu Ferries
w virtuferries.com

GETTING AROUND BY SCOOTER

Rental Motor Bike
w rentalmotorbike.com

GETTING AROUND BY BICYCLE

BiciPa
w bicipa.it

Practical Information

Passports and Visas

Visitors from outside the European Economic Area (EEA), European Union (EU) and Switzerland need a valid passport to travel to Italy, as do UK visitors. Swiss, EEA and EU nationals can use identity cards instead. Visitors from Canada, the US, Australia and New Zealand can stay for up to 90 days without a visa, as long as their passport is valid for 6 months beyond the date of entry. A visa is necessary for longer stays and must be obtained in advance from the Italian embassy (Schengen visas are valid). All other visitors need valid passports and visas. For details, check the **Ministero degli Esteri** website.

The **UK** and **US** have a consular presence in Palermo, while most other countries, including **Australia**, have embassies in Rome.

Customs and Immigration

For EU citizens there are no limits on most goods taken in or out of Italy, as long as they are for personal use only. Exceptions include firearms and weapons, endangered species and some types of food and plants. Cash amounts over €10,000 taken into or out of the EU must be declared.

Non-EU residents can claim back sales tax (VAT) on purchases over €155; have your Tax Free forms from the store ready at the airport.

Travel Safety Advice

Visitors can get up-to-date travel safety information from the **UK Foreign and Commonwealth Office**, the **US Department of State** and the **Australian Department of Foreign Affairs and Trade**.

Travel Insurance

It is advisable to take out insurance for medical emergencies, including repatriation, cancellations or delays, theft or loss of belongings. Some of these are included with your airline ticket so check when you book.

Italy has a reciprocal health agreement with other EU countries, and EU citizens are entitled to free emergency treatment if they are holders of a valid **European Health Insurance Card (EHIC)**. However, visitors have to pay for any prescriptions upfront. Italy has a reciprocal agreement with **Australian Medicare** as well, but all other nationals should check before travelling.

Health

Hospitals with accident and emergency departments include Palermo's **Villa Sofia**, **Policlinico Paolo Giaccone** and **Ospedale Civico**, and Catania's **Ospedale Garibaldi** and **Ospedale Cannizzaro**. Hotels will also be able to suggest English-speaking doctors and dentists.

Vaccinations are not necessary when visiting Italy, and there are few health hazards in Sicily. During summer, you should wear a hat and sunscreen, stay out of the sun at peak times, and drink plenty of fluids. Tap water is fine but you may prefer the taste of bottled water. Mosquitoes can be bothersome: spray exposed skin with repellent in the evenings and keep windows closed when the lights are on in your room. If bitten, ask a pharmacist for an antihistamine cream such as Fargan or Polaramin. When swimming in the sea it's wise to wear a jellyfish repellent; if stung wash the area with sea water and use a pain killer.

Pharmacies are marked with a green cross and sell common drugs, without a prescription. *Parafarmacie* have a blue or red cross and sell over-the-counter medicines, toiletries and baby formula, and are open on Saturdays. If you run out of your regular medicine, pharmacists may sell replacements, if you have the packaging.

Medical and first aid stations known as the **Guardia Medica Turistica** set up at seaside resorts in Palermo and Catania and work 24 hours a day.

Personal Security

Sicily is a relatively safe place to visit, and even in big cities such as Palermo or Catania, violence is rare. However, it is always good to be aware of your surroundings at all times.

During the day, leave valuables and documents at the hotel, and use a cross-body bag. At night, walk only in well-lit areas, and if feeling unsure, call a taxi to get back to the hotel. At the beach, do not leave your belongings unattended while you're out swimming.

Drinking in excess is generally frowned upon, although parts of the historic centre such as La Vucciria in Palermo or Porta Uzeda in Catania can get rowdy at night. Though larger cities are generally well policed, pickpocketing is quite common, especially on crowded buses and at popular tourist sites. Be firm if approached and asked for money.

Italy has two police forces. The **Carabinieri** are the military branch and have major stations in **Catania**'s Piazza Verga and **Palermo**'s Piazza Verdi. The **Polizia di Stato** are the civil branch and have their headquarters *(questura)* in **Palermo**'s Piazza della Vittoria and **Catania**'s Piazza Santa Nicolella. Crimes can be reported to either, and both can issue crime or loss reports *(denuncia di furto o smarrimento)*. There are hotlines for the **fire brigade** as well as for the **ambulance**. All calls to police and emergency services are free, whether from landlines, mobile phones or pay phones.

Women, especially solo travellers, can expect to attract attention, particularly in smaller towns. Open staring, cat calls and verbal flirtation are common and annoying although harmless, and instances of assault are very rare. If you do find yourself in a threatening situation, be firm and scream *"aiuto!"* (help) if needed to fend off a would-be assailant.

DIRECTORY

PASSPORTS AND VISAS

Australian Embassy
Via Bosio Antonio 5, Rome
🌐 italy.embassy.gov.au

British Honorary Consulate
c/o S Tagliavia & Co, Via Cavour 117, Palermo
🌐 ukinitaly.fco.gov.uk

Ministero degli Esteri
🌐 vistoperitalia.esteri.it/home/en

US Consular Agency
Via Vaccarini 1, Palermo
🌐 it.usembassy.gov/embassy-consulates/naples/

TRAVEL SAFETY ADVICE

Australian Department of Foreign Affairs and Trade
🌐 dfat.gov.au
🌐 smartraveller.gov.au

UK Foreign and Commonwealth Office
🌐 gov.uk/foreign-travel-advice

US Department of State
🌐 travel.state.gov

TRAVEL INSURANCE

Australian Medicare
🌐 humanservices.gov.au/customer/dhs/medicare

European Health Insurance Card (EHIC)
🌐 nhs.uk/ehic

HEALTH

Guardia Medica Turistica, Catania
Viale Kennedy
📞 335 530 3085

Guardia Medica Turistica, Palermo
Via Regina Elena 73/75
📞 091 6841264

Ospedale Cannizzaro, Catania
Via Messina 829
📞 095 7261111

Ospedale Civico, Palermo
Piazza Nicola Leotta 4
📞 091 6661111

Ospedale Garibaldi, Catania
Via Palermo 636
📞 095 7591111

Policlinico Paolo Giaccone, Palermo
Via del Vespro 129
📞 091 6551111

Villa Sofia, Palermo
Piazza Salerno 1
📞 091 7801111

PERSONAL SECURITY

Ambulance
📞 118

Carabinieri
📞 112
🌐 carabinieri.it

Carabinieri, Catania
Piazza Verga 8
📞 095 537999
🌐 carabinieri.it

Carabinieri, Palermo
Piazza G Verdi
📞 091 587533
🌐 carabinieri.it

Fire Brigade
📞 115

Polizia di Stato
📞 113
🌐 poliziadistato.it

Polizia di Stato Questura, Catania
Piazza Santa Nicolella 8
📞 095 7367111
🌐 poliziadistato.it

Polizia di Stato Questura, Palermo
Piazza della Vittoria 8
📞 091 210111
🌐 poliziadistato.it

Disabled Travellers

Sicily is not yet entirely accessible to disabled travellers because conservation laws prevent alterations to its many old buildings, although some have had wheelchair-accessible ramps added. Major museums and galleries have disabled facilities and many hotels have converted a few rooms to be accessible.

For the most part, public transport is wheelchair accessible. For more information and to plan your trip, visit the **Sicilia Accessibile** website.

Currency and Banking

Italy is among the 19 European countries using the euro (€), which is divided into 100 cents. Banknotes come in denominations of €5, €10, €20, €50, €100, €200 and €500. Coins are 1c, 2c, 5c, 10c, 20c, 50c, €1 and €2.

The easiest way of getting cash is with a debit card from a cash machine (ATM), which is known as a Bancomat in Italy. Most debit cards will allow a maximum daily withdrawal of €250. Bank branches are usually open 8:30am–1:30pm Monday to Friday and then again for an hour at some point between 2:30pm and 4pm, though many might not be open in the afternoon before a major holiday. Banks are also closed the feast day of a town's patron saint.

Pre-paid currency cards (cash passports) are a secure way of carrying money. They can be preloaded with euros, fixing the exchange rate before you leave, and then used in the same way as a debit card. The maximum daily withdrawal limit is usually €700. **Thomas Cook** offers these, as do most banks.

Many shops accept chip and pin cards, and almost all hotels and restaurants now accept credit cards.

Internet and Telephone

Fast-speed Internet and free Wi-Fi is available in many cafés and hotels across Sicily; occasionally the password will be posted for all patrons to see, or you can ask the proprietor. Some cities also provide free Wi-Fi, with all of the hotspots clearly marked.

European and Asian mobile phones work in Italy, but Americans will need a triband phone. Your home provider will have roaming options, but check rates carefully before you leave. A cheaper alternative may be to purchase an Italian SIM card, available at all major phone shops. However, you will need to show ID to buy one.

The main Italian mobile operators are Vodafone, TIM, 3 and Wind. You can buy rechargeable SIM cards for €10, including €5 of credit. They can be topped up at tobacconists with a SISAL terminal (used for playing lottery games), by buying a scratch card (from newsagents and tobacconists) or in the phone company's own shops. Some large chain supermarkets also sell top-up cards.

If you want to use a public telephone to make a call, you will need to purchase a phone card (scheda telefonica) from a newsagent or tobacconist. Several kinds of phone card are available for international calls – the best value is the Carta Insieme (€5).

Postal Services

The Italian postal system, **Poste Italiane**, can be appallingly slow. If you need to use it, avoid sending registered mail as it tends to accumulate at the collection point before being sent on. If speed is of the essence for destinations within Italy, use the postal system's courier service, Paccocelere, or for international destinations use a private courier such as **DHL** or **UPS**.

Stamps (francobolli) can be purchased at post offices and tobacconists, and occasionally at shops selling postcards.

Newspapers and Radio

For information about Sicilian news in English pick up a copy of **Times of Sicily**, also available online. Some social media sites have groups devoted to expat life in Sicily and are invaluable resources of information.

International magazines and newspapers are easy to find in Palermo, but they can be expensive and may well be out of date, meaning that online news sources are far better value. For general Italian news in English try the **Life In Italy** website.

Opening Hours

The days when Sicily's sights shut down for *riposo* (the long lunch break), or even the entire afternoon, are fast becoming history, as is the custom of shutting down on Sundays – a recent law states that businesses can now stay open both during lunchtime and on Sundays.

Most major museums and sights stay open all day, as do an increasing number of supermarkets and international chain stores, with some shops in Palermo staying open around the clock.

Shops, churches and other businesses that still follow tradition will usually open at 8am or 9am, close at 12:30 or 1pm, open again at 3pm or 4pm (or 5pm in summer), and close at some point between 6pm and 8pm. Many museums, art galleries and archaeological sites are closed on Monday. Their opening times vary widely – always check before starting out. Last admission to many visitor attractions is an hour before closing time.

Time Difference

Italy operates on Central European Time (CET), an hour ahead of Greenwich Mean Time (GMT), 6 hours ahead of Eastern Standard Time (EST), 9 hours ahead of Pacific Standard Time (PST) and 9 hours behind Australian Eastern Standard Time (AEST). The clock moves forward 1 hour during Daylight Saving Time from the last Sunday in March to the last Sunday in October.

Electrical Appliances

The electricity supply in Italy is 220 volts. Italian plugs come with two and three round pins, so an adaptor is sometimes necessary – ask for one that will fit both types of plug socket.

Driving

To hire a car in Italy you generally need to be over 18 years old and have held a full driving licence for at least one year. The law requires all car-hire companies to restrict vehicle choice according to the number of years you've had a licence, so don't expect to be able to hire a sports car if you've been driving for less than three years.

When you pick up the vehicle, you will need to show your passport, a credit card from which to pay the security deposit and an IDP (International Driving Permit), which is required by Italian law. Check whether the car-hire fee include insurance.

Weather

Sicily has a typical Mediterranean climate. The summer heat can be oppressive in inland towns, with cooler temperatures in the mountains. Winters are mild, but snowfall can be copious in mountainous areas. Spring's middle ground keeps hotels booked, although it can also be very blustery; autumn is also popular, but prone to downpours.

High season stretches from Easter to July and then from September to October. The majority of the shops and restaurants in the larger cities are closed throughout August because this is when local residents head off to the beaches or mountains to escape the searing heat.

Visitor Information

Visitor information offices can be found at all four airports in Sicily, where staff can be helpful with giving suggestions on where to stay; they will also hand out as many free maps as you need.

There are several tourist information points that are dotted around Palermo and Catania, often designated with an "I"; in smaller cities tourist information offices are often called Pro Loco.

Trips and Tours

Regardless of whether you are a first-time visitor or a seasoned traveller, seeing all the sights the island has to offer in a short amount of time can be a daunting experience.

To maximise your time and have a memorable stay, put your trip in the hands of a local tour company, who will have decades of experience in devising practicable, personalized guided tours, depending on the length of your visit. They can also arrange extras such as transport, airport transfers and lodgings. **Sicilytravel** is a leading company in planning day excursions as well as multiday tours all over the island. It will also provide custom tours with the focus on special-interest subjects such as genealogical research, visiting the sites of the Allied landing, or tracing the Jewish history of Sicily. **Sunway** offers tours and excursions to renowned sights and little-known jewels off the beaten track that only an insider would be aware of, as well as specialized trips on local gastronomy or folklore. Sunway is also one of the very few companies that offer guided tours of the Aeolian Islands. Besides English, both companies will offer tours in other languages, if requested.

Shopping

Ceramics are the best thing to purchase in Sicily, but bringing them home can be a problem as they're heavy and can break if poorly packed. Most ceramic shops ship overseas, though prices can be exorbitant. Taking a few bottles of wine and olive oil is also a good idea – producers will ship to anywhere. High street and designer fashion is rarely cheaper than back home, but fabulous bargains can be found in stock houses and outlets such as **Sicilia Outlet Village** near Enna, which sells last season's overstock and seconds. Sales in Sicily run from January to March and again from July to September.

Haggling is expected in markets, but hardly ever in shops, and never in high-end shops or in department stores. When haggling, be ready to go through the full ritual, including acting less and less interested, while the merchant acts ever more offended and claims he can go no lower.

Italy's Value Added Tax (VAT) is a sales tax already added on to the sticker price of every item. If you are a non-EU resident and spend more than €155 in a single shop, you can get the tax refunded. Ask the store to help you fill out the forms, then take these along with the receipts to the customs office at the airport of the last EU country you'll be visiting to complete the paperwork. Your refund will be posted but it may take months. Stores with signs saying "Tax-Free Shopping for Tourists" speed up the process, giving you a cheque for the customs office to stamp, which you redeem at the airport's Tax-Free Shopping desk.

Dining

Eating out is a way of life in Sicily, and families often meet at restaurants for their Sunday meals. The traditional meal consists of an antipasto (starter), *primo* (pasta, rice or soup), *secondo* (meat or fish), *contorno* (vegetable) and *dolce* (dessert), and until recently, tourists ordering only a salad would be treated with disdain. But international eating habits have arrived, and most places – especially in the larger cities – no longer expect diners to spend two hours over a five-course meal. Menus have freed up, and many places advertise themselves as serving "easy food", meaning that the menus are designed for diners to choose from, whatever the time of day.

Only traditional restaurants now open solely at lunch and dinner. Waiters generally expect you to linger over your meal, and won't rush you.

Most restaurants charge for bread and cover, and if the menu says *"servizio incluso"*, it means the service charge is built in. If not, tip a discretionary 10 per cent. Jacket and tie are almost never required.

Where to Stay

Sicily has a great range of memorable places at which to stay – opulent hotels, chic boutique hideaways and a variety of B&Bs, apartments and hostels.

Location is hugely important: staying in a city centre can put all conveniences at your fingertips, but can often be expensive. Make sure you do your homework on the area around the hotel before booking: what can be described as an "edgy neighbourhood" may mean insalubrious and noisy. Staying at an *agriturismo* is peaceful, but more often than not you will need a vehicle to go into town. Some resort hotels are closed in the winter, but those that are open can be real bargains in the off-season months.

Based on a checklist of facilities, Italian hotels are given an official rating of between one and five stars. However, these star ratings are no guide to the other attractions of a hotel, such as the decor or the friendliness of staff. Popular websites such as **TripAdvisor** and **Booking.com** can help with suggestions, reviews and actual bookings.

Over the past decade, since a law was passed to allow ordinary people to offer bed-and-breakfast facilities in their homes, hundreds of B&Bs have opened up everywhere: **BBPlanet, Hotels.com** and the **Associazione Nazionale Bed and Breakfast Italiani** will help you find and book one. The nicest ones offer excellent value for money, with charming, helpful owners and fantastic breakfasts. Many of these establishments do not have staff in the same building, which may not necessarily be a disadvantage, but be sure to ask how to contact the owner should the need arise. It's also a good idea to check whether breakfast is included in the rate, and if guests are allowed the use of the kitchen.

Sites such as **Airbnb** have made it easy for owners to offer their home for short holiday rentals, whether that is a simple, functional city-centre crash-pad or a glamorous apartment on the *piano nobile* of a historic *palazzo*. **The Thinking Traveller** website is a good resource for those wanting to rent out a whole villa. Several religious organizations also offer accommodation, not solely to the religious. These may, however, have a curfew at night and be open only to one gender. Prices are not necessarily low, but they can be a good option for anyone nervous about travelling alone.

Rates and Booking

Booking sites and hotel websites often offer huge discounts on standard rates as it is common for prices to be adjusted according to demand. The best deals are usually found online and well in advance. Smaller hotels' websites are not always secure, and it is unwise to email credit card details to them – finalise the booking over the phone.

All hotels in major tourist destinations on the island (from five-star hotels and flats to rented rooms and even campsites) are by law obliged to add the city tourist tax to their rates; this can be anything from €1 to €7 per night so always check if it is included in the rate that has been quoted to you. The tax is charged for a maximum of 10 nights. It's also important to keep a vigilant eye out for hidden costs: some hotels still charge for Wi-Fi, although it is worth using your powers of persuasion to get it waived. Making a phone call from a hotel room is always expensive, but phone cards usually work from hotels. If the hotel has blocked the freephone number, there will generally be a local access number on the phone card as well that can be used. Most B&Bs do not have phones for guest use, although some will offer their guests rechargeable SIM cards.

DIRECTORY

TRIPS AND TOURS

Sicily Travel
W sicilytravel.net
C 360 397 9930

Sunway
W sunway.it
C 347 185 6950

SHOPPING

Sicilia Outlet Village
W siciliaoutletvillage.com

WHERE TO STAY

Airbnb
W airbnb.it

Associazione Nazionale Bed and Breakfast Italiani
W anbbi.it

BBPlanet
W bbplanet.com

Booking.com
W booking.com

Hotels.com
W it.hotels.com

The Thinking Traveller
W thethinkingtraveller.com

TripAdvisor
W tripadvisor.com

Places to Stay

PRICE CATEGORIES

For a standard, double room per night (with breakfast if included), taxes and extra charges.

€ under €100   €€ €100–€200   €€€ over €200

Luxury Hotels

Eremo della Giubiliana, Ragusa

MAP F5 ▪ Contrada da Giubiliana ▪ 093 2669119 ▪ Dis. access ▪ www.eremodellagiubiliana.it ▪ €€

This elegant 15th-century monastic building has 13 rooms, six suites and five cottages, meaning that each of its guests receives attentive service. Rooms, public areas and grounds are authentically restored with wood and iron furnishings, fountains and stone courtyards.

Locanda Don Serafino, Ragusa Ibla

MAP F5 ▪ Via XI Febbraio 15 ▪ 093 2220065 ▪ www.locandadonserafino.it ▪ €€

Some of this hotel's 12 rooms are carved out of the rocky cliffside to which Ibla clings. The hotel offers distinctive rooms and a private lido at Marina di Ragusa.

La Moresca Maison de Charme, Marina di Ragusa

MAP F6 ▪ Via Dandolo 63 ▪ 093 2239495 ▪ www.lamorescahotel.com ▪ €€

This gorgeous neo-Gothic building, a few metres from the sea, has plush rooms with period pieces. Offers a superb buffet breakfast. Open April to November.

Excelsior Palace Hotel, Taormina

MAP H3 ▪ Via Toselli 8 ▪ 094 223975 ▪ www.excelsiorpalacetaormina.it ▪ €€€

A four-star hotel known for its views of Etna, its gardens and swimming pool are on a ridge overlooking the Bay of Naxos.

Grand Hotel Baia Verde, Catania

MAP G4 ▪ Via Angelo Musco 8/10, Aci Castello ▪ 095 491522 ▪ www.baiaverde.it ▪ €€€

The 147 rooms and 10 suites are all renovated, with living areas and a terrace. They surround the palm-filled pool area and look out to sea.

Grand Hotel Timeo & Villa Flora, Taormina

MAP H3 ▪ Via Teatro Greco 59 ▪ 094 26270200 ▪ www.belmond.com/it/grand-hotel-timeo-taormina ▪ €€€

Located in the palm- and bougainvillea-covered hillside below Taormina's ancient Greek theatre. The 70 rooms are in Baroque style. The restaurant and bar occupy terraces with amazing views.

Grand Hotel Villa Igiea, Palermo

MAP L2 ▪ Salita Belmonte 43 ▪ 091 6312111 ▪ Dis. access ▪ www.villa-igiea.com ▪ €€€

Art Nouveau architect Ernesto Basile built this grand villa at the end of the 19th century on the slopes of Monte Pellegrino. Dine on the terraces overlooking the sea.

El Jebel, Taormina

MAP H3 ▪ Salita Ciampoli 9 ▪ 094 2625494 ▪ www.hoteleljebel.com ▪ €€€

Hidden away off Corso Umberto, El Jebel is an exquisite five-star hotel with eclectic interiors and a rooftop lounge boasting sweeping views over the ocean. The on-site restaurant, Ciampoli, is one of Taormina's best.

San Domenico Palace, Taormina

MAP H3 ▪ Piazza San Domenico 5 ▪ 094 2613111 ▪ Dis. access ▪ www.san-domenico-palace.com ▪ €€€

Built as a monastery in the 1400s, San Domenico Palace now houses 105 rooms and offers views of the bay and Mount Etna, a fitness room, beauty area, a pool and gym.

Terre di Vendicari, Noto

MAP G5 ▪ Contrada Vaddeddi ▪ 346 359 3845 ▪ www.terredivendicari.it ▪ €€€

There are just four rooms, in calming white and ochre, in these luxuriously renovated farm buildings. Nestle into one of the four-poster beds on the terrace and follow the line of the swimming pool out to the sea on the horizon. Service is attentive.

Historic Hotels

Baglio Spanò, Petrosino, near Marsala
MAP B3 ▪ Contrada Triglia Scaletta ▪ 348 882 2095 ▪ www.bagliospano. com ▪ €
A gorgeous country house from the 1800s set in citrus groves, with six traditionally decorated rooms and a restaurant serving excellent food.

Grand Hotel et des Palmes, Palermo
MAP L3 ▪ Via Roma 398 ▪ 091 6028111 ▪ Dis. access ▪ www.hotel-despalmes.it ▪ €
Built in the mid-1800s and later converted to Art Nouveau style, this hotel has columned, marbled public spaces and a gym.

Hotel Relais Modica
MAP G6 ▪ Via Tommaso Campailla 99 ▪ 093 2754 451 ▪ www.hotelrelais modica.it ▪ €
This renovated *palazzo* offers lovely views of Modica, a roof garden and family rooms. The service is friendly.

Massimo Plaza, Palermo
MAP L4 ▪ Via Maqueda 437 ▪ 091 325657 ▪ www. massimoplazahotel.com ▪ €
A renovated *palazzo* with soundproofed rooms and views of the piazza. The stairs are steep and there is no lift. On-site parking.

Atelier sul Mare, Castel di Tusa
MAP E2 ▪ Via Cesare Battisti 4 ▪ 092 1334295 ▪ www.ateliersulmare.it ▪ €€
Of the 40 rooms here, 20 are Art Rooms, each an installation piece created by a modern artist. Each has a seafront terrace.

Foresteria Baglio della Luna, Agrigento
MAP D4 ▪ Via S A Guastella 1C, Valle dei Templi ▪ 092 2511061 ▪ www.baglio dellaluna.com ▪ €€
Guests are made to feel at home in this restored 13th-century watch-tower and 18th-century villa. The bright central courtyard here leads onto terraces shaded by olive and fruit trees with views out to Agrigento's famed temples (*see pp32–5*). Rooms on the upper level are furnished with antiques.

Giardino sul Duomo, Ragusa
MAP F5 ▪ Via Capitano Bocchieri 24 ▪ 093 2682 157 ▪ Dis. access ▪ www. giardinosulduomo.it ▪ €€
This historic building, set in fine gardens, offers lovely views over Ragusa's cathedral and town centre to the hills and valleys beyond. The 12 large rooms are elegant.

Hotel Belvedere, Taormina
MAP H3 ▪ Via Bagnoli Croci 79 ▪ 094 223791 ▪ www.villabelvedere.it ▪ €€
This was built as a grand hotel on Taormina's hill-side in 1902. Renovations have modernized the guest rooms without losing their original charm (most have good views). The Belvedere is also noted for its pleasant gardens with citrus and palm trees and serves lunches beside the pool. The hotel is open from March to November.

Il Principe Hotel, Catania
MAP G4 ▪ Via Alessi 20/26 ▪ 095 2500345 ▪ www.ilprincipehotel. com ▪ €€
This carefully renovated Baroque-style building is set in the historic heart of Catania. Rooms offer every modern comfort and, for additional luxury, there is a Turkish bath for guests to enjoy.

Hotel L'Ariana, Rinella, Salina
MAP G1 ▪ Via Rotabile 11 ▪ 090 9809075 ▪ www. hotelariana.it ▪ €€€
This whimsical villa was built onto the rocks above the tiny port of Rinella at the turn of the 20th century and has long been in the same family. Rooms are simple, and the best ones are those on the first floor, which open onto a terrace with great views.

Villa Athena, Agrigento
MAP D4 ▪ Via Passeggiata Archeologica 33 ▪ 092 2596288 ▪ www.hotel villaathena.it ▪ €€€
A hotel and spa within the Valley of the Temples, it offers grand rooms, some with private terraces, and is the only place on the island where you can swim and play tennis with the temples as a backdrop.

Resort Hotels

Approdo di Ulisse, Favignana
MAP A3 ▪ C/da Calagrande ▪ 092 3921 125 ▪ www.aurum hotel.it ▪ €€
A tastefully designed resort of whitewashed bungalows and cottages by a series of tiny caves

on the west side of the island. Pool, tennis and diving available.

La Dimora di Spartivento, Ragusa
MAP F5 ▪ SS 115, Km 323 ▪ 093 21865377 ▪ www.dimoradispartivento.it ▪ €€
In a rural setting with views over the Hyblean plateau and Modica to the sea, this hotel has 16 big, comfortable rooms and a pool with a small waterfall.

Kalura Hotel, Cefalù
MAP E2 ▪ Via Vincenzo Cavallaro 13 ▪ 092 1421 354 ▪ www.hotel-kalura.com ▪ €€
A modern hotel with 72 rooms and a range of facilities, including a pool, private beach, billiard tables, tennis courts and mountain bikes. Sailing and horse riding trips can also be organized. Kalura Hotel is open from mid-March to mid-November.

Il Piccolo Etna Golf Hotel & Resort, Castiglione di Sicilia
MAP G3 ▪ SS 120, Km 200 ▪ 094 2986384 ▪ www.ilpiccoloetnagolfresort.com ▪ €€
This resort is located on the slopes of Mount Etna with an 18-hole golf course, pool, tennis courts, gym and spa.

Atlantis Bay, Taormina Mare
MAP H3 ▪ Via Nazionale 161 ▪ 094 2618011 ▪ www.atlantisbay.it ▪ €€€
A luxurious hotel with full-service spa and private beach. The pool and terrace for dining are at the water's edge and the elegant rooms

have a private terrace with views of the bay.

Capofaro Malvasia & Resort, Salina
MAP G1 ▪ Via Faro 3 ▪ 090 9844330 ▪ www.capofaro.it ▪ €€€
Eighteen luxurious rooms with balconies open onto sea views at the Tasca d'Almerita family's five-star resort. Whitewashed buildings are set off by splashes of bougainvillea.

Grand Hotel Minareto, Syracuse
MAP H5 ▪ Via del Faro Massolivieri 26 ▪ 093 1721222 ▪ www.grandhotelminareto.it ▪ €€€
In the natural Plemmirio reserve, this resort has a spa, pools, private beach and two restaurants.

Hotel Villa Sant' Andrea, Taormina
MAP H3 ▪ Via Nazionale 137, Taormina Mare ▪ 094 26271200 ▪ Closed Oct–Apr ▪ www.hotelvillasantandrea.com ▪ €€€
The rooms here have terraces, offering wonderful sea views, and are set in a restored 19th-century villa beneath Monte Tauro.

Raya, Panarea
MAP G1 ▪ Via San Pietro ▪ 090 983013 ▪ Closed Nov–Mar ▪ www.hotelraya.it ▪ €€€
This place is a study in relaxation, where whitewashed buildings with large terraces look out to the sea. There is a restaurant right over the water serving fresh fish dinners on a terrace lit with oil lamps. Children under 12 are not allowed.

Verdura Resort, Sciacca
MAP C4 ▪ SS 115, Km 131 ▪ 092 5998001 ▪ Dis. access ▪ www.roccofortehotels.com/hotels-and-resorts/verdura-resort ▪ €€€
A top-class resort with its own stretch of coastline, three golf courses and a spa. Its location makes it suitable for trips to Agrigento and Selinunte.

Comfortable Hotels

Albergo Maccotta, Trapani
MAP B2 ▪ Via Degli Argentieri 4 ▪ 092 328418 ▪ www.albergomaccotta.it ▪ €
The Albergo Maccotta boasts an excellent location in Trapani's historic centre. Rooms are basic and clean.

Centrale Palace Hotel, Palermo
MAP L5 ▪ Via Vittorio Emanuele 327 ▪ 091 336 666 ▪ Dis. access ▪ www.eurostarhotels.co.uk ▪ €
An elegant, restored *palazzo* with luxurious marble-clad public areas. Guests can enjoy romantic dinners and splendid views on the roof terrace.

Hotel Il Barocco, Ragusa Ibla
MAP F5 ▪ Via Santa Maria La Nuova 1 ▪ 093 2663 105 ▪ www.ilbarocco.it ▪ €
Rooms are comfortable at this centrally located hotel, the staff are helpful, parking is available and there is a breakfast room on site. This is a great base for exploring southeast Sicily.

Hotel Miramare, Selinunte

MAP B4 ■ Via Pigafetta 2 ■ 092 446666 ■ Dis. access ■ www.hotel miramareselinunte.it ■ €

The charming Miramare hotel overlooks the Mediterranean sea, and affords a breathtaking view of the nearby Acropolis of Selinute. The hotel has its own private beach, piano bar and pizzeria restaurant. It also provides WiFi and private parking.

Hotel Pomara, San Michele di Ganzaria

MAP F4 ■ Via Vittorio Veneto 84 ■ 093 3976976 ■ Dis. access ■ www. hotelpomara.com ■ €

The Pomara is one of the most comfortable inland options. The location is rustic with views of the rolling hills, though the hotel itself is modern. It has an excellent restaurant, and is convenient for visiting Enna, Piazza Armerina, Morgantina and Caltagirone.

Hotel Posta, Palermo

MAP L3 ■ Via Antonio Gagini 77 ■ 091 587338 ■ www.hotelposta palermo.it ■ €

This three-star hotel is an excellent bargain option in Palermo. There are 27 large, clean rooms, the public areas have TVs, and parking is available. The hotel is situated near the church of San Domenico.

Katane Palace Hotel, Catania

MAP G4 ■ Via Finocchiaro Aprile 110 ■ 095 7470702 ■ www.katanepalace.it ■ €

This modern hotel has 60 spacious rooms in a

renovated *palazzo* just steps from one of the city's daily markets and the chic Via Etnea. Helpful staff, an elegant bar and an on-site restaurant. There is parking available, but book in advance.

Hotel Aegusa, Favignana

MAP A3 ■ Via Garibaldi 11 ■ 092 3921638 ■ Dis. access ■ www.aegusa hotel.it ■ €€

Book a stay here for its modern rooms, a terrace and a small garden restaurant, all tucked away in Favignana town.

Hotel del Corso, Taormina

MAP H3 ■ Corso Umberto I, 238 ■ 094 2628698 ■ www.hoteldelcorso taormina.com ■ €€

A three-star hotel that is recommended by locals. The modern rooms have small terraces with good views, overlooking the hillside, the Bay of Naxos and Mount Etna. Street parking is available.

Hotel Elios, Taormina

MAP H3 ■ Via Bagnoli Croci 98 ■ 094 223431 ■ www.elioshotel.com ■ €€

A family-run hotel below the Teatro Antico, Hotel Elios features comfortable and spacious rooms, and almost all have full or partial sea views. It also has a rooftop with lounge chairs in which to relax.

Hotel Gutkowski, Syracuse

MAP H5 ■ Lungomare di Levenate 26 ■ 093 1465 861 ■ Dis. access ■ www. guthotel.it ■ €€

In summer, breakfast is served on the terrace at

this hotel on the Ortygia seafront. The hotel has its own wine bar.

Relais Antiche Saline, Paceco

MAP B2 ■ Via Gerdi, Località Nubia ■ 092 386 8042 ■ Inx.relaisantiche saline.it/site ■ €€€

A renovated historic building with spacious rooms offering views over the Egadi Islands and the saltpans of Trapani's coast. There are also a pool area, an outdoor spa with a Finnish sauna and a good restaurant. Transport to Trapani upon request.

Agriturismo and B&Bs

Baglio Fontanasalsa, Trapani

MAP B2 ■ Via Cusenza 78 ■ 092 3591001 ■ www. fontanasalsa.it ■ €

This lovely *agriturismo* is a working olive farm on an 18th-century property, with rustic rooms, citrus orchards and play spaces for children.

Sotto i Pini, Zafferana Etnea

MAP G3 ■ Via A Diaz 208, Pisano ■ 095 956696 ■ www.sottoipini.it ■ €

A charming Art Nouveau villa set in its own vineyards, olive groves and orchards, offering views of Mount Etna and the sea. Breakfast features organic, seasonal, local produce, much of it home-grown.

Torre di Renda, Piazza Armerina

MAP E4 ■ Enna, Piazza Armerina ■ 093 5680208 ■ www.torrerenda.it ■ €

This rustic *agriturismo* in the hills around Piazza

For a key to hotel price categories see p142

Armerina has spacious rooms. Horse riding and bicycle tours available. There is a swimming pool and restaurant on site.

La Zagara, Furci Siculo

MAP H3 ▪ Via Manzoni 5 ▪ 338 229 7864 ▪ www. lazagarabeb.it ▪ €
In a village near Taormina, just steps from the beach, the five rooms here have private bathrooms and balconies with sea views.

BB 22, Palermo

MAP M3 ▪ Via Pantelleria 22 (junction Largo Cavalieri di Malta) ▪ 091 326214 ▪ www. bb22.it ▪ €€
Each guest room in this centrally located B&B in a restored *palazzo* is unique. Expect feather tassels on the gilt bureau, hot-pink terry-covered bath furniture as well as armoires decorated with lovely Eastern motifs.

Locanda COS, Vittoria

MAP F5 ▪ SP3, Km 14,300 ▪ 338 960 8713 ▪ www. cosvittoria.it ▪ €€
Restored farmhouses on the grounds of the COS winery have been turned into romantic apartments with high domed ceilings and balconies. Gorgeous pool area, winery tours available on request and traditional food.

Mandranova, Palma di Montechiaro

MAP D5 ▪ SS 115, km 217 ▪ 393 986 2169 ▪ www. mandranova.com ▪ €€
Producing award-winning olive oil, Mandranova is nestled between the sea and the coastline, where old farmhouses have been converted into 13 rooms

and four suites. On-site facilities include a small pool, reading room, pool hall and cooking courses. Two-night minimum stay.

Masseria Susafa, Polizzi Generosa

MAP E3 ▪ Contrada Susafa ▪ 338 960 8713 ▪ www. masseriasusafa.com ▪ €€
This converted farmhouse in the Madonie mountains has a rustic glamour. The 13 rooms accommodate anywhere from two to six people. On-site restaurant.

Talìa, Modica

MAP G6 ▪ Via Exaudinos 1/9 ▪ 093 2752075 ▪ www.casatalia.it ▪ €€
Small stone houses in Modica's ancient ghetto have been sensitively renovated and linked via original terraced gardens and stone staircases. The rooms are minimally decorated with Sicilian materials.

Self-Catering and Villas

Agrituristica Villa Levante, Castelbuono

MAP E3 ▪ Via Isnello ▪ 092 1671914 ▪ www. villalevante.it ▪ €
Three nicely restored self-catering apartments are set in the towers of a 19th-century castle with pretty gardens and a farm producing olive oil. There are marked trails for a walk to Castelbuono, hiking and mountain biking.

Apartments Casa Giudecca, Cefalù

MAP E2 ▪ Via Candeloro 127 ▪ 092 1922339 ▪ www.bookingcefalu. com ▪ €
Apartments for rent to the east of Cefalù. Built on a

cliffside, with balconies overlooking the sea, and steps down the cliffs.

B&B Enza Marturano, Lipari

MAP G1 ▪ Via Maurolico 35 ▪ 368 322 4997 ▪ No credit cards ▪ www. enzamarturano.it ▪ €€
In the centre of Lipari, not far from the Marina Corta, this place features four bright private rooms with cooking facilities. Rooms are grouped around a communal sitting room, kitchen and terrace.

Sicily Holiday Rentals

093 21961701 ▪ www. sicilyholidayrentals.com ▪ €€
Carefully selected villas in the countryside, or apartments by the sea, are offered through this company, which specializes in properties in Pozzallo, but also lists places in Ragusa and Syracuse.

Pensione and Monasteries

La Giara, Nicolosi

MAP G3 ▪ Viale della Regione 12/a ▪ 095 791 9022 ▪ www.giara.it ▪ €
Spacious rooms and colourful decor make this place an appealing base for exploring Mount Etna. There is an ample terrace with views up to the volcano.

Il Giardino del Barocco, Noto

MAP G5 ▪ Via Aurispa Giovanni 77 ▪ 093 1573 919 ▪ www.ilgiardinodel barocco.it ▪ €
This small *pensione* is set in a magnificent historic palace with a courtyard garden, offering an oasis of calm in the city centre.

Monastero di San Benedetto, Modica

MAP G6 ▪ Via Santa Maria e Sant'Antonio 7 ▪ 093 2941033 ▪ No credit cards ▪ No air conditioning ▪ €

A few minutes' walk from the station, this monastery, founded in 1892, has single bedrooms and a refectory. It is mainly for religious retreats.

Pensione Tranchina, Scopello

MAP C2 ▪ Via A Diaz 7 ▪ 092 4541099 ▪ www.pensionetranchina.com ▪ €

A 10-room *pensione* in a tiny fishing village, with decorated rooms that have iron or wooden bedsteads; several have a sea view. The owners cook excellent Sicilian cuisine, mainly using fresh seafood and garden vegetables.

SoleLuna della Solidarietà, Palermo

MAP L2 ▪ Via Vincenzo Riolo 7 ▪ 091 581671 ▪ Dis. access ▪ No credit cards ▪ www.solelunabedandbreakfast.org ▪ €

Each room here has its own private, though not en-suite, bathroom. The owner donates 5 per cent of her proceeds to a local youth group; she also offers tours of Palermo.

Albergo Domus Mariae, Syracuse

MAP H5 ▪ Via Vittorio Veneto 76 ▪ 093 124854 ▪ www.domusmariaebenessere.com ▪ €€

The Ursuline sisters run a modern hotel in a restored 19th-century *palazzo* on Ortygia. All 16 rooms have air conditioning; some have a sea view. Book in advance.

Pocho, San Vito lo Capo

MAP B2 ▪ Localita Isulidda ▪ 092 3972525 ▪ Dis. access ▪ www.hotel-pocho.it ▪ €€€

A small *pensione* with 12 comfortable rooms, some decorated with items from a traditional Sicilian puppet theatre. There is a terrace restaurant, sea views and a beach nearby.

Campsites and Hostels

Baia dei Coralli, Palermo

MAP D2 ▪ Via Plauto 27, Sferracavallo ▪ 091 77850 80 ▪ www.aighostels.it ▪ €

Just a few steps from the beach in a seaside resort, this hostel sleeps 76 in double or four-bed rooms. It's a short bus ride from Palermo.

Camping Baia Unci, Lipari

MAP G1 ▪ Via Marina Garibaldi 3/7, Canneto ▪ 090 9811909 ▪ www.campingbaiaunci.it ▪ €

Set on a beautiful bay on the island of Lipari, this well-shaded campsite takes tents, campervans and caravans. Also available are fully furnished, air-conditioned bungalows for 2–6 people.

Camping Costaponente, Cefalù

MAP E2 ▪ Loc. Ogliatrillo, state road 113, Km 190 ▪ 092 1420085 ▪ No credit cards ▪ www.campingcostaponente.com ▪ Closed Nov–Mar ▪ €

A three-star campsite with spots for tents and caravans, a swimming pool, tennis courts and access to the beach below. Its facilities include a bar, small market and self-service restaurant.

Camping La Focetta Sicula, Sant'Alessio Siculo

MAP H3 ▪ Contrada Siena 40 ▪ 094 2751657 ▪ www.lafocetta.it ▪ €

Located right by the sea, this campsite has 85 beds in furnished bungalows and mobile homes with air conditioning, heating and with a shaded terrace or veranda.

Il Forte Camping Village, Marzamemi

MAP G6 ▪ Contrada Spinazza ▪ 093 1841011 ▪ Dis. access ▪ www.ilfortevillage.it ▪ €

This camping village with bungalows and parking is located near a sandy beach. Facilities include public telephones, a bar, restaurant and market, as well as diving, boat, bike and scooter hire.

Ostello Degli Elefanti, Catania

MAP G4 ▪ Via Etnea 28 ▪ 095 2265691 ▪ www.ostellodeglielefanti.it ▪ €

Set in a 17th-century *palazzo*, just steps from Piazza Duomo, this hostel offers dorms and private rooms, a reading room, kitchen and a rooftop terrace with views of Mount Etna.

Taormina's Odyssey, Taormina

MAP H3 ▪ Via Paterno di Biscari 13 ▪ 094 224533 ▪ Dis. access ▪ www.taorminaodyssey.com ▪ €

There's a very friendly atmosphere at this hostel in the residential part of Taormina, a short walk from the centre. Private rooms or dormitory.

For a key to hotel price categories see p142

Index

Acknowledgments

Author
Elaine Trigiani is a Sicilian-American art historian living in Italy since 1998. A certified olive-oil taster, she designs and leads travel programmes, as well as running cooking classes in Sicily, Tuscany and the US.

Additional contributor
Conchita Vecchio

Publishing Director Georgina Dee

Publisher Vivien Antwi

Design Director Phil Ormerod

Editorial Ankita Awasthi Tröger, Rebecca Flynn, Rachel Fox, Maresa Manara, Scarlett O'Hara, Sally Schafer, Farah Sheikh

Cover Design Richard Czapnik.

Design Marisa Renzullo, Vinita Venugopal

Commissioned Photography Amanda Heywood, Demetrio Carrasco, Nigel Hicks, Bridget Williams

Picture Research Subhadeep Biswas, Taiyaba Khatoon, Sumita Khatwani, Ellen Root

Cartography James McDonald, Casper Morris, Animesh Pathak, John Plumer

DTP Jason Little

Production Igrain Roberts

Factchecker Toni DeBella

Proofreader Kathryn Glendenning

Indexer Helen Peters

Illustrator Chris Orr & Associates
chrisorr.com

First edition created by Sargasso Media Ltd, London

Picture Credits
The publisher would like to thank the following for their kind permission to reproduce their photographs:
Key: a-above; b-below/bottom; c-centre; f-far; l-left; r-right; t-top

123RF.com: Giuseppe Anello 54clb, 75tr; Yury Dmitrienko 99cr; lsantilli 81tr.

Le 4 Stagioni, Menfi: 105bc.

4Corners: Antonino Bartuccio 14br, 16cl, 17tl, 28-9, 36-7, 80bl, 87cla; Gabriele Croppi 121b; Giorgio Filippini 17crb; Johanna Huber 25crb; SIME / Paolo Giocoso 13tl, 13c, 16br, 22-3, 73cla; Alessandro Saffo 4cra, 26t, 48tl, 84b, 113tl; Stefano Scatà 79bc; Sebastiano Scattolin 24-5.

Accursio: 79cr.

Alamy Stock Photo: Arcaid Images 45tr; Bon Appetit 122tl; Dennis Cox 35br; Cultura Creative 3tr, 132-3; Stephen Emerson 18-9; EmmePi Travel 71tr; Giulio Ercolani 7tr, 125t; Findlay 19br; funkyfood London / Paul Williams 15tr, 19tl, 20-1; Hemis 31bl; Horizons WWP / TRVL 115cra; imageBROKER 14-5, 69tr, 96tl; Ingolf Pompe 86 72b; Ivy Close Image 120clb,; Yadid Levy 50t; LOOK Die Bildagentur der Fotografen GmbH 97clb; Marshall Ikonography 120ca; Angus McComiskey 33tl; Sandro Messina 114tl; Giovanni Montella 115cb; Francesco Palermo 50bl; Photo 12 57tr; Photolocate 6c; Massimo Piacentino 28bl, 125crb; Domenico Piccione 14cl, 53cl; Realy Easy Star / Toni Spagone 28crb, 29cr, 81cl, 82t; REDA &CO srl 34crb, 34bl, 61cra; Rolf Richardson 10tr; robertharding 1; Rolf Nussbaumer Photography / Stefan Huwiler 10crb; Romas_ph 92cra; Roberto Lo Savio 2tl, 8-9; Peter Scholey 35t, 36bl, 51c; Neil Setchfield 29tl; Ivan Vdovin 2tr, 4crb, 40-1; Martyn Vickery 83clb; WaterFrame 64b; Westend61 GmbH 54tr; Jan Wlodarczyk 3tl, 24br, 88-9, 106-7; Michal Zieba 67tr.

The Antonio Pasqualino International Puppet Museum: 68br

AWL Images: Neil Farrin 11tr; Hemis 65cla, 109b; Katja Kreder 4t, 60t, 100cl; Sabine Lubenow 86crb; PhotoFVG 21tl; Ken Scicluna 33crb; Marco Simoni 16-7, 46bl, 100-1.

Cantine Pellegrino, Marsala: 104tl.

Capitolo Primo: 123crb.

Le Colonne, Taormina: 82cb.

La Coppola Storta: 95c.

La Darsena da Iannuzzo, Syracuse: 131cra.

Depositphotos Inc: agiampiccolo 124tl; boggy22 30-1; elisalocci 126cl; giuliaisabella 68tl; siculodoc 30cl.

Dreamstime.com: Al1962 76tl, 81bc; Ivan Vander Biesen 47tr; Delstudio 113cr; Dianaphotography 4cla; Yury Dmitrienko 102t; Sabrina Dvihally 118tl; Ebastard129 85clb, 112b, Ellesi 103bl, Emicristea 32-3, Eugenia Struk 85tr, Marzia Giacobbe 76bl; William Giannelli 83tr; Yulia Grigoryeva 122br; Kasto80 13bl; Kityyaya 48b; Vladimir Korostyshevskiy 94cla; Lachris77 30crb, 73br, 114br; Lev Levin 38cl; Elisa Locci 24cla; Lorenzograph 77cl; Anna Lurye 6b, 10b, 18cl, 126br, 130b; Mahroch 11crb; Marcorubino 49crb; Stanisa Martinovic 45cl; Marzolino 52-3, 84tr; Mattiaath 65br; Mirekdeml 128cla; Martin Molcan 62-3; Nanisimova 110-1; Pavlinec 44tr; Ariadna De Raadt 105cl; Ralligeller 44b; Andrea G. Ricordi 103cr; Jozef Sedmak 12clb, 91br; Denise Serra 117ca; Siculodoc 69cl;

Thevirex 87br; Travelling-light 123ca; Raluca Tudor 77tr; Tupungato 116ca; Denisa Vlaicu 109cra; Vvoevale 19cr, 75cl, 77bl; Andreas Zerndl 46t.

Getty Images: Stefano Bianchetti 42b, 56t; Culture Club 53tr; De Agostini Picture Library 39crb, / Archivio J. Lange 38tr, 59b, / G. Cappellani 39b, / G. Cigolini 43cl, / G. Dagli Orti 4clb, 37cb, 42tc, 43br, / G. Nimatallah 90tl; LatitudeStock - Mel Longhurst 31tl; Claudio Lavenia 86tl; Maremagnum 59tr; Fabio Montalto 78b; Vittoriano Rastelli 57bl; Roberto Soncin Gerometta 74b; Slow Images 4cl, 11cra, 108tl; UniversalImagesGroup 55bl; Visuals Unlimited, Inc. / Richard Roscoe 21crb.

Internazionale delle Marionette Pasqualino, Palermo: Dorling Kindersley / Demetrio Carrasco 51tr.

iStockphoto.com: alxpin 12-3; Brzozowska 4b, 98ca; eddygaleotti 91tr; eZeePics Studio 76c; helovi 52tl; JannHuizenga 55tr; Krivinis 118b; kruwt 127cl; lucamato 38c; master2 60bl, 94b; Rolf_52 95tr; RolfSt 11bl; ROMAOSLO 92-3; SalvoV 11tl; Satephoto 58cl; vladj55 119cla; VoeVale 20cla, 117br.

I Luoghi del Lavoro Contadino, Buscemi: 129tr.

Majore, Chiaramonte Gulfi: 78cla.

Museo Geologico Gemellaro, Palermo: 66cla.

Opera dei Pupi di Enzo Mancuso, Palermo: 71b.

Regione Siciliana -Dipartimento dei Beni Culturali e dell'Identità Siciliana: 26br, 27tr, 27cl, 27br.

Robert Harding Picture Library: Sabine Lubenow 11clb, 110bl, 111cl; Matthew Williams-Ellis 64tl.

SuperStock: Art Archive 56crb; Cubo Images 74cla; Cubo Images / Giuseppe Greco 128br; DeAgostini 37tl; age fotostock / Mike Randolph 80tr; imageBROKER 72tl, /Martin Moxter 70clb,; Melvyn Longhurst 101tl; Marka 67cla; Travel Library Limited 32cla.

Cover

Front and spine: **Alamy Stock Photo:** Jan Wlodarczyk.

Back: **123RF.com:** Anna Lurye.

Pull Out Map Cover

Alamy Stock Photo: Johnny Stockshooter.

All other images © Dorling Kindersley

For further information see:
www.dkimages.com

As a guide to abbreviations in visitor information blocks: **Adm** = *admission charge;* **DA** = *disabled access;* **D** = *dinner;* **L** = *lunch.*

Printed and bound in China

First published in Great Britain in 2003 by Dorling Kindersley Limited 80 Strand, London WC2R 0RL

Copyright 2003, 2018 © Dorling Kindersley Limited

A Penguin Random House Company

18 19 20 21 10 9 8 7 6 5 4 3 2 1

Reprinted with revisions 2005, 2007, 2009, 2011, 2013, 2015, 2018

A CIP catalogue record is available from the British Library.

ISBN 978 0 2413 0918 6

SPECIAL EDITIONS OF DK TRAVEL GUIDES

DK Travel Guides can be purchased in bulk quantities at discounted prices for use in promotions or as premiums. We are also able to offer special editions and personalized jackets, corporate imprints, and excerpts from all of our books, tailored specifically to meet your own needs.

To find out more, please contact:

in the US
specialsales@dk.com

in the UK
travelguides@uk.dk.com

in Canada
specialmarkets@dk.com

in Australia
penguincorporatesales@ penguinrandomhouse.com.au

Phrase Book

In an Emergency

Help!	Aiuto!	eye-yoo-toh!
Stop!	Fermo!	fair-moh!
Call a doctor	Chiama un medico	kee-ah-mah oon meh-dee-koh
Call an ambulance	Chiama un' ambulanza	kee-ah-mah oon am-boo-lan-tsa
Call the police	Chiama la polizia	kee-ah-mah lah pol-ee-tsee-ah
Call the fire brigade	Chiama i pompier	kee-ah-mah ee pom-pee-air-ee

Communication Essentials

Yes/No	Sì/No	see/noh
Please	Per favore	pair fah-vor-eh
Thank you	Grazie	grah-tsee-eh
Excuse me	Mi scusi	mee skoo-zee
Hello	Buon giorno	bwon jor-noh
Goodbye	Arrivederci	ah-ree-veh-dair-chee
Good evening	Buona sera	bwon-ah sair-ah
What?	Cosa?	koh-sah?
When?	Quando?	kwan-doh?
Why?	Perchè?	pair-keh?
Where?	Dove?	doh-veh?

Useful Phrases

How are you?	Come sta?	koh-meh stah?
Very well, thank you	Molto bene, grazie	moll-toh beh-neh grah-tsee-eh
Pleased to meet you	Piacere di conoscerla	pee-ah-chair-eh dee-coh-noh-shair-lah
Where is/are …?	Dov'è/ Dove sono …?	dov-eh/doveh soh-noh?
How do I get to …?	Come faccio per arrivare a …?	koh-meh fah-choh pair arri-var-eh ah …?
Do you speak English?	Parla inglese?	par-lah een-gleh-zeh?
I don't understand	Non capisco	non ka-pee-skoh
I'm sorry	Mi dispiace	mee dee-spee-ah-cheh

Shopping

How much does this cost?	Quant'è, per favore?	kwan-teh pair fah-vor-eh?
I would like …	Vorrei …	vor-ray …
Do you have …?	Avete …?	ah-veh-teh …?
Do you take credit cards?	Accettate carte di credito?	ah-chet-tah-teh kar-teh dee creh-dee-toh?
What time do you open /close?	A che ora apre/ chiude?	ah keh or-ah ah-preh/kee-oo-deh?
this one	questo	kweh-stoh
that one	quello	kwell-oh
expensive	caro	kar-oh
cheap	a buon prezzo	ah bwon pret-soh
size (clothes)	la taglia	lah tah-lee-ah
size (shoes)	il numero	eel noo-mair-oh
white	bianco	bee-ang-koh
black	nero	neh-roh
red	rosso	ross-oh
yellow	giallo	jal-loh
green	verde	vair-deh
blue	blu	bloo

Types of Shop

bakery	il forno /il panificio	eel forn-oh /eel pan-ee-fee-choh
bank	la banca	lah bang-kah
bookshop	la libreria	lah lee-breh-ree-ah
cake shop	la pasticceria	lah pas-tee-chair-ee-ah
chemist	la farmacia	lah far-mah-chee-ah
delicatessen	la salumeria	lah sah-loo-meh-ree-ah
department store	il grande magazzino	eel gran-deh mag-gad-zee-noh
grocery	alimentari	ah-lee-men-tah-ree
hairdresser	il parrucchiere	eel par-oo-kee-air-eh
ice-cream parlour	la gelateria	lah jel-lah-tair-ree-ah
market	il mercato	eel mair-kah-toh
newsstand	l'edicola	leh-dee-koh-lah
post office	l'ufficio postale	loo-fee-choh pos-tah-leh
supermarket	il supermercato	eel su-pair-mair-kah-toh
tobacconist	il tabaccaio	eel tah-bak-eye-oh
travel agency	l'agenzia di viaggi	lah-jen-tsee-ah dee vee-ad-jee

Sightseeing

art gallery	la pinacoteca	lah peena-koh-teh-kah
bus stop	la fermata dell'autobus	lah fair-mah-tah dell ow-toh-booss
church	la chiesa la basilica	lah kee-eh-zah lah bah-seel-i-kah
closed for holidays	chiuso per le ferie	kee-oo-zoh pair leh fair-ee-eh
garden	il giardino	eel jar-dee-no
museum	il museo	eel moo-zeh-oh
railway station	la stazione	lah stah-tsee-oh-neh
tourist information	l'ufficio di turismo	loo-fee-choh dee too-ree-smoh

Staying in a Hotel

Do you have any vacant rooms?	Avete camere libere?	ah-veh-teh kah-mair-eh lee-bair-eh?
double room	una camera doppia	oona kah-mair-ah doh-pee-ah
with double bed	con letto matrimoniale	kon let-toh mah-tree-moh-nee-ah-leh
twin room	una camera con due letti	oona kah-mair-ah kon doo-eh let-tee
single room	una camera singola	oona kah-mair-ah sing-goh-lah
room with a bath/shower	una camera con bagno, con doccia	oona kah-mair-ah kon ban-yoh, kon dot-chah
I have a reservation	Ho fatto una prenotazione.	oh fat-toh oona preh-noh-tah-tsee-oh-neh

Eating Out

Have you got a table for …?	**Avete una tavola per …?**	ah-veh-teh oona tah-voh-lah pair …?
I'd like to reserve a table	**Vorrei riservare una tavola**	vor-ray ree-sair-vah-reh oona tah-voh-lah
breakfast	**la colazione**	lah koh-lah-tsee-oh-neh
lunch	**il pranzo**	eel pran-tsoh
dinner	**la cena**	lah cheh-nah
the bill	**il conto**	eel kon-toh
waitress	**cameriera**	kah-mair-ee-air-ah
waiter	**cameriere**	kah-mair-ee-air-eh
fixed price menu	**il menù a prezzo fisso**	eel meh-noo ah pret-soh fee-soh
dish of the day	**il piatto del giorno**	eel pee-ah-toh dell jor-no
starter	**antipasto**	an-tee-pass-toh
first course	**il primo**	eel pree-moh
main course	**il secondo**	eel seh-kon-doh
vegetables	**contorni**	eel kon-tor-noh
dessert	**il dolce**	eel doll-cheh
cover charge	**il coperto**	eel koh-pair-toh
wine list	**la lista dei vini**	lah lee-stah day vini
glass	**il bicchiere**	eel bee-kee-air-eh
bottle	**la bottiglia**	lah bot-teel-yah
knife	**il coltello**	eel kol-tell-oh
fork	**la forchetta**	lah for-ket-tah
spoon	**il cucchiaio**	eel koo-kee-eye-oh

Menu Decoder

l'acqua minerale	lah-kwa mee-nair-ah-leh gah-zah-tah/ nah-too-rah-leh	mineral water fizzy/still
gassata naturale		
'agnello	lah-niell-oh	lamb
l'aglio	lal-ee-oh	garlic
al forno	al for-noh	baked
alla griglia	ah-lah greel-yah	grilled
la birra	lah beer-rah	beer
la bistecca	lah bee-stek-kah	steak
il burro	eel boor-oh	butter
il caffè	eel kah-feh	coffee
la carne	la kar-neh	meat
carne di maiale	kar-neh dee mah-yah-leh	pork
la cipolla	la chip-oh-lah	onion
i fagioli	ee fah-joh-lee	beans
il formaggio	eel for-mad-joh	cheese
il fritto misto	eel free-toh mees-toh	mixed fried dish
la frutta	la froot-tah	fruit
frutti di mare	froo-tee dee mah-reh	seafood
i funghi	ee foon-ghee	mushrooms
i gamberi	ee gam-bair-ee	prawns
il gelato	eel jel-lah-toh	ice cream
l'insalata	leen-sah-lah-tah	salad
il latte	eel laht-teh	milk
il manzo	eel man-tsoh	beef
l'olio	loh-lee-oh	oil
il pane	eel pah-neh	bread
le patate	leh pah-tah-teh	potatoes
le patatine fritte	leh pah-tah-teen-eh free-teh	chips
il pepe	eel peh-peh	pepper
il pesce	eel pesh-eh	fish
il pollo	eel poll-oh	chicken
il pomodoro	eel poh-moh-dor-oh	tomato
il prosciutto	eel pro-shoo-toh	ham
il riso	eel ree-zoh	rice
il sale	eel sah-leh	salt
la salsiccia	lah sal-see-chah	sausage
il succo d'arancia/ di limone	eel soo-koh dah-ran-chah/ dee lee-moh-neh	orange/lemon juice
il tè	eel teh	tea
la torta	lah tor-tah	cake/tart
l'uovo	loo-oh-voh	egg
vino bianco	vee-noh bee-ang-koh	white wine
vino rosso	vee-noh ross-oh	red wine
le vongole	leh von-goh-leh	clams
lo zucchero	loh zoo-kair-oh	sugar
la zuppa	lah tsoo-pah	soup

Numbers

1	**uno**	oo-noh
2	**due**	doo-eh
3	**tre**	treh
4	**quattro**	kwat-roh
5	**cinque**	ching-kweh
6	**sei**	say-ee
7	**sette**	set-teh
8	**otto**	ot-toh
9	**nove**	noh-veh
10	**dieci**	dee-eh-chee
11	**undici**	oon-dee-chee
12	**dodici**	doh-dee-chee
13	**tredici**	tray-dee-chee
14	**quattordici**	kwat-tor-dee-chee
15	**quindici**	kwin-dee-chee
16	**sedici**	say-dee-chee
17	**diciassette**	dee-chah-set-teh
18	**diciotto**	dee-chot-toh
19	**diciannove**	dee-chah-noh-veh
20	**venti**	ven-tee
30	**trenta**	tren-tah
40	**quaranta**	kwah-ran-tah
50	**cinquanta**	ching-kwan-tah
60	**sessanta**	sess-an-tah
70	**settanta**	set-tan-tah
80	**ottanta**	ot-tan-tah
90	**novanta**	noh-van-tah
100	**cento**	chen-toh
1,000	**mille**	mee-leh
2,000	**duemila**	doo-eh mee-lah
1,000,000	**un milione**	oon meel-yoh-neh

Time

one minute	**un minuto**	oon mee-noo-toh
one hour	**un'ora**	oon or-ah
a day	**un giorno**	oon jor-noh
Monday	**lunedì**	loo-neh-dee
Tuesday	**martedì**	mar-teh-dee
Wednesday	**mercoledì**	mair-koh-leh-dee
Thursday	**giovedì**	joh-veh-dee
Friday	**venerdì**	ven-air-dee
Saturday	**sabato**	sah-bah-toh
Sunday	**domenica**	doh-meh-nee-kah